Violent Femme

Praise for the series:

It was only a matter of time before a clever publisher realized that there is an audience for whom *Exile on Main Street* or *Electric Ladyland* are as significant and worthy of study as *The Catcher in the Rye* or *Middlemarch* ... The series ... is freewheeling and eclectic, ranging from minute rock-geek analysis to idiosyncratic personal celebration—*The New York Times Book Review*

Ideal for the rock geek who thinks liner notes just aren't enough—*Rolling Stone*

One of the coolest publishing imprints on the planet—*Bookslut*

These are for the insane collectors out there who appreciate fantastic design, well-executed thinking, and things that make your house look cool. Each volume in this series takes a seminal album and breaks it down in startling minutiae. We love these. We are huge nerds—*Vice*

A brilliant series ... each one a work of real love—*NME* (UK)

Passionate, obsessive, and smart—*Nylon*

Religious tracts for the rock 'n' roll faithful—*Boldtype*

[A] consistently excellent series—*Uncut* (UK)

We ... aren't naive enough to think that we're your only source for reading about music (but if we had our way ... watch out). For those of you who really like to know everything there is to know about an album, you'd do well to check out Bloomsbury's "33 1/3" series of books—*Pitchfork*

For almost 20 years, the 33-and-a-Third series of music books has focused on individual albums by acts well known (Bob Dylan, Nirvana, Abba, Radiohead), cultish (Neutral Milk Hotel, Throbbing Gristle, Wire) and many levels in-between. The range of music and their creators defines "eclectic," while the writing veers from freewheeling to acutely insightful. In essence, the books are for the music fan who (as Rolling Stone noted) "thinks liner notes just aren't enough."—*The Irish Times*

For reviews of individual titles in the series, please visit our blog at 333sound.com and our website at http://www.bloomsbury.com/musicandsoundstudies

Follow us on Twitter: @333books

Like us on Facebook: https://www.facebook.com/33.3books

For a complete list of books in this series, see the back of this book.
Forthcoming in the series:

Shout at the Devil by Micco Caporale
I'm Wide Awake, It's Morning by Holden Seidlitz
Tragic Kingdom by Rhae Lynn Barnes
Believe by Lior Phillips
Weird Al Yankovic in 3-D by Justin Remer
I'm Your Baby Tonight by Brandon Tensley
Plastic Beach by Ihor Junyk
Disintegration by Andi Harriman
Dust Bowl Ballads by Allison C. Meier
Blonde by Yousef Srour
Lyburnum Wits End Liberation Fly by Zak Fusciello
What's the 411 by Ricky Tucker
and many more …

Violent Femmes

Nic Brown

Illustrations by Kacey Nicosia

BLOOMSBURY ACADEMIC

NEW YORK · LONDON · OXFORD · NEW DELHI · SYDNEY

BLOOMSBURY ACADEMIC
Bloomsbury Publishing Inc, 1359 Broadway, New York, NY 10018, USA
Bloomsbury Publishing Plc, 50 Bedford Square, London, WC1B 3DP, UK
Bloomsbury Publishing Ireland, 29 Earlsfort Terrace, Dublin 2, D02 AY28,
Ireland

BLOOMSBURY, BLOOMSBURY ACADEMIC and the Diana logo are
trademarks of Bloomsbury Publishing Plc

First published in the United States of America 2026

Bloomsbury Publishing Inc does not have any control over, or responsibility
for, any third-party websites referred to or in this book. All internet addresses
given in this book were correct at the time of going to press.
The author and publisher regret any inconvenience caused if addresses
have changed or sites have ceased to exist, but can accept no
responsibility for any such changes.

Library of Congress Control Number: 2026931238

ISBN: PB: 979-8-7651-3351-4
           ePDF: 979-8-7651-3353-8
          eBook: 979-8-7651-3354-5

Series: 33 1/3

Typeset by Integra Software Services Pvt. Ltd.
Printed and bound in the United States of America

For product safety related questions contact
productsafety@bloomsbury.com.

To find out more about our authors and books visit www.bloomsbury.com
and sign up for our newsletters.

For Shannon Ferguson

Contents

Prologue: The Organist   1

Formation   9
The Instruments   21
The Studio   43
The Songs   51
Release and Success   99

Epilogue: In Dreams Begin Responsibilities   113

Acknowledgments   122
Sources   123

Prologue: The Organist

You know the song, but you can't place it.

Maybe it's because you're inside of a baseball stadium. It isn't a setting in which you often think about music. Or maybe it's because the melody in question is being played by an organist, or because it's hot and you're in direct sun. Whatever the problem is, you can't figure it out, but then you don't have a chance to think much more about it because almost as soon as the melody has started—after just sixteen staccato notes over three short measures—it ends, at which point every human in the stadium claps two short bursts of double sixteenth notes in response.

All day long the guy on the organ has been cranking out the classics. "If You're Happy and You Know It," "The Mexican Handclapping Song," "Take Me Out to the Ball Game," "Charge." None of these songs has made you think about much of anything. They're just empty signals to cheer. But this one, the song the organist has just started up again, it conjures a distinctly different feeling for you, something more potent and strange, something personal, something deep and nostalgic and formative. Something important. Something that has something to do with art.

There it is. It's coming back to you now, at first as an image.

You see a glowing doorway.

You're eleven years old, standing before it.

It's 1988.

You're at Doug Starr's house after school, and there is a melody issuing forth from that doorway of light. You've been drawn to the sound like some hypnotized preteen moth to the flame. And it's the same song you're hearing right now, only in your memory it isn't being played by an organist. No, it's being performed on some type of guitar that sounds like it's getting pecked at by an angry bird, and there's a young man singing above that guitar in a thin, high voice, dancing just along the edge of breaking. It's all issuing forth from a small boombox on the top of a dresser, and then you realize you're looking into Doug's older sister's bedroom, because suddenly there she is: maybe sixteen years old, pulling a sweater from a drawer. She's bent over and her blond hair is hanging like a curtain into a sunbeam. It glows in that light, perhaps even brighter than the sun itself. And the song, you realize, as you listen closely, is even *about* the sun. It's about … a blister in the sun?

"What is this?" you say.

Doug's sister looks up. Somehow she understands you're asking about the music, even though you haven't said as much. The power of the song makes the point moot.

"It's the Violent Femmes," she says.

Back in the stadium you point to air.

"It's the Violent Femmes!" you say.

"Oh, yeah," your wife says. "Weird."

It is weird. How did this happen? How did *this* song— "Blister in the Sun," the opening track off the acoustic post-punk band's self-titled 1983 debut—manage to enter the American lexicon of sporting anthems? The band who wrote it, after all, is a group of Midwestern art weirdos who straddle the rarely converging realms of punk, folk, and jazz, a Bermuda Triangle of musical influences for anyone, let alone a stadium organist. Nonetheless here it is, "Blister in the Sun," sounding out like a clarion call to the lolling outfielders and screaming hot dog vendors and pale sunburning grandpas.

You look around and wonder what this means about yourself, what it means about the country and its culture, and even what it means about time in general, to discover that the counterculture anthem of your youth has now become the soundtrack for America's pastime. But then you stop thinking and clap.

Released on April 13, 1983, the self-titled debut from Milwaukee's Violent Femmes arrived to scant sales or attention. Led by a then nineteen-year-old singer and songwriter named Gordon Gano, the band was so iconoclastic—performing a type of highly literate jazz-influenced punk music on instruments better suited for a jug band (Mariachi-style bass, guitar, and a metal bucket and snare drum played with brushes by a drummer who stood)—that it couldn't even engender support from Milwaukee's anti-establishment punk scene. For years, the band performed almost exclusively on street corners, simply because they couldn't get a gig.

In a way, it's incredible that the Violent Femmes' first album got made, or that the band found someone to release it. But that's only one angle on this album's singular story. Another way of looking at it is to say that the album was an inevitable product of unique genius, that once its songs were written, there was no way anything could ever really stop them from spreading, with tapes passing reverently from listener to listener for years as the album slowly gained traction on college radio and in dorm rooms and on car stereos and on Walkmen until 1991, when it snuck onto the bottom of the Billboard Top 200, eight years after its release, at which point it had already quietly gone gold and then platinum and in the process changed the lives of millions of young people and artists and musicians.

Like me.

I play the drums. My own high school band performed "Blister in the Sun" a few times, just like every other high school band in the world. Unlike most high school bands, though, mine ended up signing a record deal with Atlantic Records just after graduation and went on to score a top 20 Billboard alternative rock hit in 1998. ("What I Didn't Know" by Athenaeum, which reached #14—you don't remember it.) In the years I spent touring with that group and others, I performed for tens of thousands of people, appeared on *The Tonight Show*, and shared the stage with bands at the top of the charts. Very few of those shows remain in my memory. One afternoon in 1998 stays crystal clear, though. It was the first of May in Atlanta, and the line-up was wildly incongruous. Along with my own band, the roster included David Byrne, Son Volt, and I think even Tito Puente, among many others. I saw none of those acts. We'd been on tour for so long by that point that I was usually more interested in napping if we had hours off. There was one other band on the bill, though, and I wasn't going to miss them for the world: the Violent Femmes. I'd listened to their debut album so many times that it felt like a part of my soul.

I stood far off stage right. I remember how the light came in from the west, throwing shadows. I remember how Brian Ritchie, the bass player, was so much taller than I had expected. How Gano was dressed in clothes that—dare I say it—looked comfortable. How the drummer played standing up. That all the band members seemed sort of weird (and not necessarily like, cool weird, but like actually weird). That they all stood in a line at the front of the stage. Together, it seemed to add up to some type of proof that these guys weren't playing by the same rules as any of the other bands I'd been sharing stages with. No, the Violent Femmes appeared to have come from somewhere else entirely, somewhere purely authentic and strange and impenetrable.

Later, backstage, I said nothing to the members. I stayed at a distance.

And then a year or two after that, on the street in New York, I walked past Brian Ritchie. I was sure it was him. He carried what I guessed was a large flute in a case on his back, and I stopped in my tracks as he passed. There is no story beyond that. I just turned and watched. I remember it like it just happened. It was like watching a piece of myself.

The point is, the Violent Femmes have haunted me ever since I discovered them that fateful afternoon at Doug Starr's house when I was eleven. Back then, their debut album didn't sound like anything I'd ever heard. It still doesn't sound like anything else. *Violent Femmes* somehow exists both outside of time and as one of the most evocative and enduring artifacts of the alternative '80s. This book, I hope, will go down as its permanent record.

First, though, I had to write it, so I got Gordon Gano on the phone. We talked through the album for hours, dissecting it, poring over each song for the purposes of these very pages, and then near the end of our conversation, I brought up some Violent Femmes tour dates that the band had scheduled near where I live. I told Gano I was planning to go to one.

"Maybe you shouldn't come," Gano said.

"Why?" I said.

"Because we play the songs differently each night," Gano said. "And you know the record so well … When you hear us live, it'll never sound right."

I got quiet for a few seconds.

"I'm joking!" Gano said.

"Yeah … " I said.

But Gano had a point. I've read enough classics—and seen enough time travel movies—to understand that anyone trying to turn back the clock runs the risk of ending up face down in the pool like Jay Gatsby. And yet here I was, focusing on the minutia of a musical moment captured more than forty years in the past. Nevertheless, after we got off the phone, I looked at their tour dates. One of the concerts was scheduled for Symphony Hall in Atlanta, with the full Atlanta Symphony backing the band. Maybe this would be the right show to go to, I thought, because—since there was nothing even close to a symphony on the actual recording—the concert would be its own thing entirely. There would be nothing for me to try to go back to.

I texted the band's management to put me on the list. Then I started writing this book. I spoke to band members, managers, the producer, other musicians. Months passed. Finally, it came time for me to go to the show. I stopped at a Dunkin' Donuts near the highway and typed in the address for Symphony Hall. Only then did I realize that what I was doing was planning a trip to Atlanta, the same city in which I'd last seen the Violent Femmes play. I almost laughed. It appeared that, despite my best efforts, I was indeed going back.

1

Formation

The night before Rufus King High School was scheduled to hold its 1981 National Honors Society induction ceremony, seventeen-year-old senior Gordan Gano was out at a punk club. The place was a dump. It was called the Starship, and it's said that sometimes in winter the heat wouldn't even come on in the place and you could find turds frozen in the toilet. Still, Gano was happy to be there. He was one of the students set to be honored at the next day's ceremony, but that didn't stop him from going out on a school night. He liked to listen to music and be a part of the scene. In fact, Gano had been writing songs of his own since he was nine years old and had just performed some of them as a solo opening act for Jonathan Richman at the Metropole Theatre a few nights before. It was one of Gano's first real gigs, and while there, he'd met another local musician, Brian Ritchie, who Gano now saw in the Starship tonight.

Gano had an idea. Rufus King High was staging a type of talent show as part of the National Honors Society ceremony in the morning. Maybe Ritchie would play it with him.

"I'm playing at my school tomorrow," Gano said. "Would you like to join me?"

Ritchie was twenty years old. Already he was a working musician. He lived on his own in his own apartment, had a day job sorting books at the Milwaukee Public Library, and was cultivating a solid identity as what he calls a "dedicated bohemian." His was a life far removed from Rufus King High School. Still, Ritchie was interested in Gano as a songwriter and had actually attended that Jonathan Richman concert the other night specifically to hear Gano play, after the theater's owner, Robert Soffian, had given Ritchie a tip. "You gotta check this kid out," Soffian had said. "He's a pint-sized Lou Reed imitator. You'll like him."

Ritchie had liked him. And so, despite the age difference and the fact that Gano was asking him to perform at a high school first thing in the morning—a time of day Ritchie was generally unacquainted with—Ritchie said yes.

"And yeah," Ritchie says, of what transpired next, "we went to the school and basically almost caused a riot."

They must have looked like opposites as they walked into the auditorium. Gano was dressed in a suit and tie, standing five-foot four, while Ritchie, who's a six-one beanpole, was decked out in the Milwaukee "punk uniform" of torn jeans and a paisley shirt.

"I want to introduce you to my music teacher," Gano said, and as soon as Ritchie saw the guy, he recognized him. It was Mr. Kalfus, Ritchie's own high school music teacher from a different school a few years before.

"He looked at me and he was like, oh no," Ritchie says. "Because he knew when I walked in that trouble was brewing."

With the whole school watching, Gano and Ritchie began their performance with "Good Friend"—a tender midtempo number that would eventually appear on the Violent Femmes' third album, 1986's *The Blind Leading the Naked*—but then, perhaps hoping to drum up some more energy, Gano switched gears and launched into "Gimme the Car."

"Come on, Dad, gimme the car," Gano sang. "I tell ya what I'm gonna do. I'm gonna pick her up. I'm gonna get her drunk. I'm gonna make her cry. I'm gonna get her high. I'm gonna make her laugh." By the chorus, as Gano was repeating the line "she can touch me all over my body," the audience, Ritchie says, went insane.

"The principal was on the side of the stage," he says. "He was waving his arms like 'Stop! Stop!' Like we were going to stop. No, we weren't going to stop. We kept going."

Gano was not inducted into the National Honor Society that morning. In fact, he fled the premises immediately after his performance and was asked to report to the principal's office along with his parents before he could return. The

National Honor Society even sent a letter requesting the return of his official lapel pin, claiming it was their property. Gano never could find that lapel pin, though he says the NHS eventually dropped the matter. More importantly, he had found a bassist.

Victor DeLorenzo was on tour with an experimental theater group in Europe at the time. The company was a Milwaukee institution called Theatre X, and they'd hired DeLorenzo to work with them as an actor after another one of their members, a local performer named Willem Dafoe, had left to pursue fame and fortune elsewhere. (He found it.) DeLorenzo, twenty-three at the time, was a musician by training—with a degree in symphonic percussion from the University of Wisconsin-Milwaukee—and so in addition to his acting work with Theatre X, he had been playing around town as a sideman. Many of those gigs had been in conjunction with Ritchie. Both were so technically excellent at their instruments that together they had found high demand for their services, and before DeLorenzo left for Europe, Ritchie had even suggested they take the highly unusual step for any rhythm section and give themselves a name.

"Brian came over one afternoon," DeLorenzo says, "and he said, 'Hey Victor, I think I came up with a name for our rhythm section: I was thinking we could call it Violent Femmes.' I said, 'Violent Femmes?' And he said, 'Yeah, well, you know how we always call people that are kind of effeminate … like the guy that can't catch the football, or talks with a lisp or something … we call them a femme?'" DeLorenzo did know what he meant—this was something like "sissy" in the parlance of

Milwaukee at the time. "And so the idea of a femme being so upset that they became violent for some reason, that struck a humorous chord in Brian's mind."

"It doesn't really matter if you like the name or not," Ritchie told him. "You're just gonna remember it because it's so odd."

Ritchie was right. The name stuck, and thus the Violent Femmes were born as a rhythm-section-for-hire before either Ritchie or DeLorenzo had ever even met Gordon Gano. Once DeLorenzo returned from Europe, though, Ritchie introduced him to the young songwriter, and DeLorenzo was struck immediately by the quality of Gano's songs.

"I mean, here's this young kid," DeLorenzo says. "The lyrical content was just masterful and massive. So even though the music might have been only three or four chords, the ideology behind it, the subtext, was very rich and thoughtful. It was well beyond someone of his years."

Gano had been writing for so many years already, though, that by the time he met DeLorenzo and Ritchie, he had written every song that would go on to appear on the first Violent Femmes album, as well as the second, and some of the third.

"In my earliest memories I was making up songs," Gano says, insisting he can still recall one that he wrote when he was nine (which he then declines to sing).

His was a house filled with music. Country, gospel, folk, cast albums, especially *Oklahoma!*, were often on the stereo, and Gano's father—a Baptist minister—and siblings all played instruments and sang. Both parents were involved in theater, and Gano's mother had even performed as a chorus girl on Broadway in the late-1940s musical *High Button Shoes*. Paperbacks were stacked so high in each room that Gano says he was literally surrounded by books as a child. It was an atmosphere of cultural sophistication. Gano was saturated with it. Still, there was no getting around the fact that he was a teenager writing songs in his bedroom, while Ritchie and DeLorenzo were both professional working musicians thriving in the Milwaukee art scene. They played jazz. They loved Sun Ra. They worked in experimental theater. They were making short films. They were basically adults involved in the highest "high art" one could really access as twenty somethings in Milwaukee at the time.

"It was a good thing that happened to Gordon," Ritchie says, of their paths crossing, "because I don't know what would have happened if he hadn't met us."

What surely would have happened is that Gano would have formed a band one way or another, but what Ritchie means, I think, is that without him or DeLorenzo, it just never would have sounded anything like Violent Femmes. For one thing, DeLorenzo and Ritchie weren't even playing the same instruments that Gano had envisioned as being part of his band.

"I would have thought that there would be two electric guitars, an electric bass, and a drum set," Gano says.

Ritchie and DeLorenzo had different ideas. The very first time they sat in with Gano—at the tiny Beneath-It-All Café, on Downer Avenue in Milwaukee—the only instruments they brought along with them were a snare drum and a banjo. On subsequent dates, Ritchie's banjo was swapped out for an acoustic bass guitar and DeLorenzo's snare drum was augmented with what he called the "tranceaphone"—a metal bushel basket turned upside down and placed over a floor tom. And while their dedication to such unusual instrumentation was in part musical, in Ritchie's case, it was also philosophical.

"I just thought that we should all be equipped to play acoustic music because there was an imminent apocalypse on the horizon," Ritchie says. "I thought we probably wouldn't have electricity. I didn't want to be caught unprepared."

Billing themselves as Gordon Gano and the Violent Femmes for their first few shows, Gano's name eventually fell away and Violent Femmes' identity firmed up. The combo that Gano had once envisioned as a four-piece electric rock band was now an acoustic trio staffed by sidemen steeped in jazz, outro folk, punk, and experimental theater.

"I thought, fine," Gano says. "You know, this sounds great, and these guys have more experience than I do."

There was an unplanned benefit to the acoustic approach. Gano's songs were impeccably crafted, to the point that they would have worked in almost any musical setting, but with such minimal instrumental framing, his vocals—and his extraordinarily evocative lyrics—rose to the surface.

"It became a strategy," Ritchie says, "like, let's play like this, and then you can hear the words. We just realized that it was an original approach and that it was something that set us apart from any of the other rock bands of that time."

The band's lineup and approach were so unusual, though, that even in the punk and experimental circles that the Violent Femmes were working within at the time, they found it hard to get gigs. It was a challenge that ended up paying off, though, because with nowhere else to play, the trio found themselves forced to busk in the streets, a practice that both reinforced the usefulness of their acoustic and lightweight instruments as well as helped shape their burgeoning stage presence.

"It was better than sitting in a damp basement trying to write material," DeLorenzo says. "It was far better to be outside on a sunny afternoon playing for the people. And that's not only how we got our own act together, that's how we got our professionalism together as far as how we were going to interact with an audience."

Some days were better than others. Sometimes people—especially children—reacted with glee. At other times, the band saw people they knew crossing the street to just get away from them. But perhaps their best day busking was when they set up outside of the Oriental Theatre on August 23, 1981. The Pretenders were playing the Oriental that night, and the line of people waiting for tickets was a perfect captive audience for the Violent Femmes, who set up beside them and started to play. Unbeknownst to the band, Peggy Sue Honeyman-Scott, wife of Pretenders guitarist James Honeyman-Scott, came outside to listen. After just a few songs, she was so impressed that she went back in and got her husband, who then invited the band to be a last-minute opener for the Pretenders that night. The Violent Femmes went on after the official opening act but before the headliner, so when the curtain came up, the crowd was expecting the Pretenders. When they saw that it was actually a band of misfits off the street, some people booed. Despite the crowd's indifference, though, the Violent Femmes could see the Pretenders on the side of the stage as they played, watching, laughing, and generally just freaking out over how good they were.

The gig itself led to nothing much tangible. There was no record deal or new onslaught of bookings or popularity. In fact, many people in the local scene resented the band because of the opportunity they'd stumbled into. More importantly, though, the show gave the Violent Femmes a rare gift of validation at a time when they needed it most.

"Brian and I had a plan that we were going to leave that particular summer and go up to Minneapolis and form a band with a friend of mine up there," DeLorenzo says. "But then once we discovered Gordon and we started playing together and we enjoyed each other's company, we decided to stay in Milwaukee and see what would happen. And luckily for us, and for the people that love Violent Femmes, that's exactly what we did."

It was around this time that a local composer and orchestral arranger, Mark Van Hecke, was walking down Downer Avenue one evening. "I was walking past a laundromat named The Wash Tub," he says, "when I heard Gordon Gano for the first time." The Wash Tub's basement, which had once been an ice cream parlor, was at the time the tiny forty-seat performance space called the Beneath-It-All Café, where the band often played. And though Van Hecke didn't know who Gano was when he heard him that night, the sound of the music drew him down the stairs. There he found Gano, Ritchie, and DeLorenzo walking around the audience while playing. At once Van Hecke recognized

DeLorenzo, who was a friend from Theatre X, where Van Hecke had composed music for several performances, and though Van Hecke had seen DeLorenzo play with other acts before—"He had a slew of bands," Van Hecke says, "and most of them were pretty bad, actually"—this one was different. The songs were incredible, and as Van Hecke watched the trio work the crowd, he thought, "This is like theater."

Soon after, Van Hecke invited the band to his apartment, where he had a recording studio set up in one of his bedrooms, and it was there that the Violent Femmes recorded their first demos. It was the band's hope that those recordings would lead them to success far beyond the street corners of Milwaukee and the walls of the Beneath-It-All Café.

"We sent them out to something like seventy or seventy-five labels," Ritchie says. "We got rejected by every label. There were a couple that were somewhat interested. I forget what they were called. One of them wanted to sign us, but they wanted us to go synth pop. It was one of these guys named Jimmy. I forget if it was Jimmy Iovine or Jimmy Ienner." Whoever it was wanted the band to rerecord versions of their songs in the vein of A Flock of Seagulls. "They were like, 'Oh, these are good songs. If we do it like that it'll be a hit.' We didn't like that idea."

"That path was never even contemplated," Gano says. "It was just like, well, no, because we know this is the way it should sound."

The band did receive legitimate interest from one person, though—Alan Betrock, a writer and producer from New York City who had worked with Blondie, the dB's, and Richard Hell and the Voidoids. Betrock had started his own label,

Shake Records, and was so enthusiastic about the Violent Femmes that he flew to Milwaukee to see the band play.

The club was abuzz that night.

"Word got out," Ritchie says, remembering how everyone in the place seemed to be looking around for the "record company guy" from New York. "It's hard to imagine nowadays what that kind of stuff meant," he says. "Back in those days, I mean, you would sell your children, your mother, grandmother, anybody just to get a whiff of a recording contract." Technology and industry were aligned in such a way that labels were essentially the only route to recording an album at the time, let alone releasing one. "There were only gatekeepers doing that," Ritchie says. "And Betrock had a label, and he wanted to do it."

Betrock liked what he saw. He met with the band and shared his enthusiasm. Things seemed to be coming together. But then Betrock developed a series of health problems soon after, and plans fell apart.

"We were so frustrated at that point that we decided to just record the album ourselves," Ritchie says.

Van Hecke wanted to continue to work with the band, and the band wanted to work with him too, but because of Van Hecke's background as a composer and conductor, some of the people in his circle felt like the pairing was a poor match.

"People were criticizing me," Van Hecke says, "saying, what the hell are you doing with these guys? I said to them, I'm going to record this album for posterity. Because I had a sense. I just felt, OK, maybe we won't be the darlings of radio, but this is going to be a unique work of art. I knew it in my heart."

The first hurdle was booking time in a real studio, because, as Van Hecke puts it, "I knew the limitations of mine." His makeshift rig consisted of a four-track recorder in a guest room, but in nearby Lake Geneva, there was a larger professional studio where Van Hecke had worked before, and he thought it would be a good option. There was one major problem, though: "It was going to cost money."

DeLorenzo was tasked with finding the funds. He was the oldest member of the band and had the most experience working out in the real world. He struck out everywhere. Out of options, he finally turned to his own father. Victor Richard DeLorenzo, a one-of-a-kind success story who had traced an incredible path for himself from barber to executive in the automobile industry, agreed to loan the band $10,000.

"Everything was at stake for us on this record," DeLorenzo says. "We had $10,000 of my father's money, which we were about to spend on something that we weren't sure was ever going to do us justice in the long run or if we were going to have to try and figure out how to pay back my dad without having a record deal."

The band had confidence. They had the right producer. They had a batch of incredible songs, and now, finally, they had enough money to go into a studio to record them. It was their hope that what they came out with would be enough to prove to everyone else what they already felt, which was that their music was something that might just change the world. What the band didn't have, though, was a record deal, or any real idea of what might happen once they managed to get one.

2

The Instruments

Before we enter the studio with the Violent Femmes, let's pause to consider the instruments that they were planning to play there. Because even if you think you understand what they were, in my experience, there's a good chance you might have it wrong. At least that was the case with me when I first heard the band's debut album. In my defense, it was the 1980s. I wasn't getting press about the band. I'd never seen a photo of the members. All I had was a dubbed cassette copy, and then later the real deal: an official tape with a cover featuring a girl peering through a window. I had no idea what the Violent Femmes looked like, let alone what their instruments looked like, or that they were unusual.

"When you're listening to the record," says Victor DeLorenzo, "it doesn't sound as unique as it is because I think the songs are so powerful."

Indeed, to a casual listener, part of the problem in getting a clear perspective on the Violent Femmes' unique instrumentation might be because their songs are so impeccably crafted—they're just so hooky and sharp—that they blind you to their presentation. It's sort of like looking at one of those Chuck Close portraits from a distance: at first you think it's a photo, but then once you get closer and see that the pixels are actually thumbprints, you realize you've been looking at something constructed from entirely different materials the whole time.

To be clear, though, in the grand scheme of things, *Violent Femmes* doesn't sound wildly unusual. There is guitar. There is bass. There are drums. There's a backbeat. There are vocals and solos and riffs. If anything, the most unconventional-sounding element at first might just be the timbre of Gano's voice. Foundationally, though, the Violent Femmes lineup is one that does not otherwise exist in popular music: an acoustic bass guitar, a guitar (sometimes acoustic, sometimes electric), and a drummer who plays a snare drum and a tranceaphone with brushes. Yet even with this information, it can still be hard to understand just how unique it all is.

"I would have to say that, in order to really possess the idea of what the Violent Femmes stand for, you need to see us play live," says DeLorenzo. "People would always have the reaction: I can't believe how much noise those guys made with just those few instruments. And I think that was one of the magical things about the Violent Femmes, that it appeared to a lot of people that we were making music out of thin air."

So let's take a look.

THE BASS

Unless you were there—and by there, I mean sixteen years old in the early 1990s and just learning how to play a musical instrument—it can be hard for people today to understand just how influential the Violent Femmes' debut album was. I think of what was happening back then as the record going viral over a span of eight years, via cassette. The burn was slow, but it was a burn nonetheless, and by the time I was a teenager, *Violent Femmes* had reached such a peak level of cultural pervasiveness that essentially everyone I hung out with, especially those of us just starting to form bands of our own, knew every note.

I was talking to my friend Shannon Ferguson about this one day when he told me a story that I think really captures things. Shannon is a guitarist and producer, best known for his work with the New York City band Longwave, but this story was about when he was sixteen years old and living in Petaluma, California, back when he was just learning to play.

"That first Violent Femmes record was so important to me," he said, and started to laugh. It was like he couldn't believe what he was getting ready to tell me. "So, when I was sixteen, I went to see the Dead Milkmen play at Slim's in San Francisco, and I found a credit card outside the theater. Credit cards were sort of new then. Or, like, not as common as they are today. Anyway, I picked it up and thought, what am going to do with this? I mean, I could have bought anything in the world with that thing. It was the golden ticket! So you know what I did? I went to a music store the next day and bought an acoustic bass guitar, because Brian Richie played one in the Violent Femmes. I could have bought anything in the world, and that's what I bought. Then I dropped the credit card down a well near my house."

It's a crazy story. I mean, I would not have used that credit card. Shannon was less law-abiding than I was at sixteen. On the other hand, it's not *that* crazy of a story. What else would any of us have bought if we could at the time? An acoustic bass guitar, the instrument Brian Ritchie played on *Violent Femmes*—that was about as close as any sixteen-year-old musician could come to touching their dreams back then. I give credit to Shannon for trying.

Another thing Shannon said that day. He said, "The weird thing about that album is that it's all lead bass." Shannon's point, I think, is that *that* was why he was buying a bass guitar in the first place, as opposed to, say, a regular guitar, but also he's right: so many of the primary instrumental melodies, hooks, and solos on *Violent Femmes* are played by Ritchie on the bass, which, to perhaps point out the obvious, is not a common state of affairs. In fact, having the bass be the lead melodic instrument on any album of popular music is pretty much unheard of.

Or maybe it isn't. Maybe we were just hearing the record the wrong way. I mean, sometimes, while listening to *Violent Femmes*, I would find myself wondering: is that even the bass? Maybe I was hearing a guitar, I would think. Or maybe something else. Or maybe I was just hearing the whole album the wrong way. So I asked Brian Ritchie.

"I mean, if you analyze it from a critical perspective," he said, "it's probably the most bass-dominated album in rock history."

OK, so, yeah, I was right.

"It's crazy," adds Victor DeLorenzo. "Because Brian is actually the lead instrument and Gordon is more of the rhythmic instrument."

Thus it's confirmed: *Violent Femmes* is indeed a platinum-selling album that's "all lead bass." It isn't a dynamic that Ritchie set out to create, though. Things just developed that way from a combination of practicality and necessity, as with so much of the Violent Femmes' sound.

"Basically," Ritchie says, explaining how he found himself in such a unique role, "my philosophy as a bass player is that you are there to do whatever anybody else is not doing. You're there to do what's required, and what was required in Violent Femmes was way different than in a normal band, where you just thump away on the root note and let everybody else fill up all the space, because Victor's drumming method was very simple. Most of the album is just a snare and the tranceaphone. And Gordon, it was the first time he was in a band, and he didn't really aspire to be like a Jimi Hendrix-style lead guitarist. He mainly likes to play rhythm guitar, and he learned a lot of that playing gospel music in church. So he's got a really good rhythmic sense. But he wasn't playing a whole lot of solos. So not only was I playing bass, but I was also filling in for the bass drum, which was not there. A lot of my lines on that album you can hear are simulating a bass drum. And then other times I would be doing the solos, which in most bands would go to the guitarist, or the keyboard player, or a sax player, or somebody else, not the bass player. So it was just because of the other guys, you know, being very minimal that I was able to be maximal."

It makes sense when Ritchie explains it like that, and it makes sense when you listen to the album, and I should mention that Ritchie is also a freakishly good musician, so he makes this whole exercise of "lead bass" seem almost effortless. But before we settle in and think, *oh, ok, this is all perfectly normal,* I want to linger a bit longer on why Ritchie's bass playing on *Violent Femmes* is so unusual, because not only is he playing "lead bass" on the whole album, he's doing it on an *acoustic bass guitar,* which probably doesn't sound too strange, because when you say acoustic bass, most people assume you're talking about a standup bass—the type of instrument you see in a jazz combo or symphony—but that isn't what Ritchie is playing. He's playing an acoustic bass guitar, a large four-string instrument that is worn around the neck and more akin to the type of thing played in a mariachi band.

It's hard for me to think of anyone else who plays this instrument exclusively. I did know this one guy when I was a teenager in the 1990s—he was a local legend for his technique, truly an incredible player—and he played one. He must have been a Brian Ritchie fan. But then he got arrested for trafficking LSD and that was the last I heard of him. The point is, there aren't too many.

For Ritchie, the instrument's draw was both sonic and practical.

"I was very much into jazz, early blues, classical music, music from around the world, and folk music," he says. "But of course I also loved the Velvet Underground, the Rolling

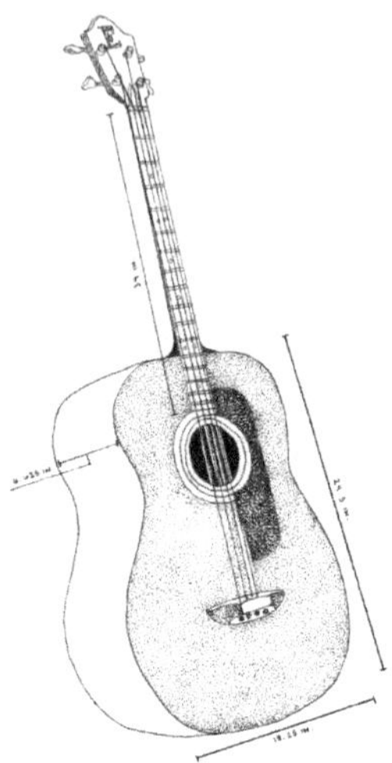

Stones, Roxy Music, T. Rex, and electric music. So I wanted to mix that energy of the electric music and punk music in with an acoustic bass. But because I didn't have a car—I didn't even have a driver's license—I wasn't going to be carting a stand-up bass around with me everywhere. So that led me to search for an acoustic bass guitar."

Ritchie tried a proof-of-concept first by converting his own acoustic guitar, which he got when he was about thirteen, to an acoustic bass guitar simply by putting some bass strings on it. This was during the time when he was already working with DeLorenzo but had yet to meet Gano.

"We were doing stuff on the street in Milwaukee with this hobo guy named Doorway Dave," Ritchie says. "He was an actual hobo. He was an actual railway dude who would like take a train from one city to another, and he'd busk for a while, and so we played with him, and that's when I was using that original acoustic bass of mine."

Ritchie's homemade acoustic bass guitar worked well enough in that context, but soon he wanted to upgrade. There's only so long you can play a cheap acoustic guitar with bass strings on it before the neck starts to pull off the body or you just tire of its crappy sound. Ritchie found two acoustic basses available on the market—one made by Guild and one by Ernie Ball. He chose the Ernie Ball model, called the Earthwood (a line that was made from the 1970s until being discontinued in 1985, after producing only around 2000 or so instruments), and he ordered one from the local shop.

"They thought I was crazy," he says.

I was discussing all this with DeLorenzo later when he asked if Ritchie had ever told the story of buying that bass guitar.

"I mean, he told me that they thought he was crazy at the store," I said, "but that was it."

"Well," DeLorenzo said. "Let me tell you a story. This is a great one. I'm surprised he didn't tell you. Anyway, Brian had seen in a magazine this Ernie Ball Earthwood bass, which was perfect for what we were looking for because it was a mariachi-style bass, but it was more of a contemporary design. So we went to our music store, called Uncle Bob's Music, and Brian was interested to see if he could put down a little bit of money to order this thing. We went in and found out that he had to put down $60, or something like that. And I think he only had $10. So we couldn't order it and we left the store and Brian was pretty bummed out. And I was sad too, because I thought, wow, this would be really cool if he can get this, this will really help with our busking on the street. So we're walking down the street, I think we're going to get the bus, and for some reason out of the corner of his eye, Brian sees this crumpled up paper bag kind of leaning underneath a bush in front of a house. And we're walking by, and I don't know why, but he just felt compelled to go over and pick up the bag. And he opened the bag and there was $55 in the bag. So he could go back and put the money down on that Ernie Ball bass."

Shannon's story of finding the credit card rose up in my mind before me, like a vision.

"Victor," I said, "you're not going to believe this."

I told him Shannon's story.

DeLorenzo got very quiet.

Things felt heavy between us in that silence, as if together we'd just received news of some great cosmic event.

"There's a lot of magic that surrounds this band," DeLorenzo said.

THE DRUMS

Now let's look at the drummer.

There he is, standing at the front of the stage between the other two band members, playing a two-piece drum set. But look closer. Not only is he missing a bass drum, the drums that he does have are really just one drum: a snare drum. That other thing is just a metal bushel basket. And there's a small cymbal too, which he barely plays. Also, he's using brushes.

I am, of course, describing Victor DeLorenzo, the only drummer who has ever fit this curious profile. DeLorenzo's drumming—and his one-of-a-kind drum set—is an integral part of the Violent Femmes' sound and foundational to how and why their debut album works the way that it does. To be clear, though, DeLorenzo's unique approach to drumming isn't anything that he ever thought he'd be doing.

"I was looking to be in the next Beatles," he says. "I wanted to play traditional drum set in a pop band."

For years he did just that, playing conventional drum set in bands around Milwaukee, as well as guitar and even singing lead in a group. The allure of standard pop music soon dulled for him, though. Remember—DeLorenzo was working as an actor in an experimental theater group at the time that the Violent Femmes formed. He had become attuned to the rewards of the unconventional.

"By the time I met Gordon," he says, "I wanted to do something a little bit more on the unique side."

Even before he met Gano, though, he had begun to explore unusual instrumentation, including coming up with the tranceaphone—the metal bushel basket DeLorenzo included in his drum set—which he invented while working on a film project with Milwaukee musician and artist Jerry Fortier, with whom he and Brian Ritchie were playing in a group called the Trance and Dance Band.

"One Saturday afternoon, we were up in Jerry's loft," DeLorenzo says. "Jerry was working on the soundtrack for a little film that he was putting together and we wanted to find something that was a percussive sound, but not necessarily something standard like a snare drum or a floor tom or a cymbal. So luckily, in the corner of Jerry's attic, he had a metal bushel basket and he had a floor tom that only had one head on it. So I mounted the floor tom on my snare drum stand and then put the metal bushel basket over the top of the floor tom, and I started to play it with metal brushes. There was a rib on the bottom of the metal bushel basket, so you could take the metal ring on the end of the brushes and you could kind of rub that on the rim of the bottom of that metal bushel basket and you'd get one kind of a sound, and then I could play with the brushes on the sides and you would get a tick sound, and then when you'd hit the center, you would get some of the resonance of the floor tom that was underneath the metal bushel basket, so that would give you kind of a thump. So you could get three distinct sounds out of that particular folk art instrument which we decided to call the tranceaphone, in homage to Jerry's Trance and Dance Band."

The tranceaphone—an utterly one-of-a-kind instrument that offered a variety of sounds suggesting conventional instrumentation—is not only a good encapsulation of the

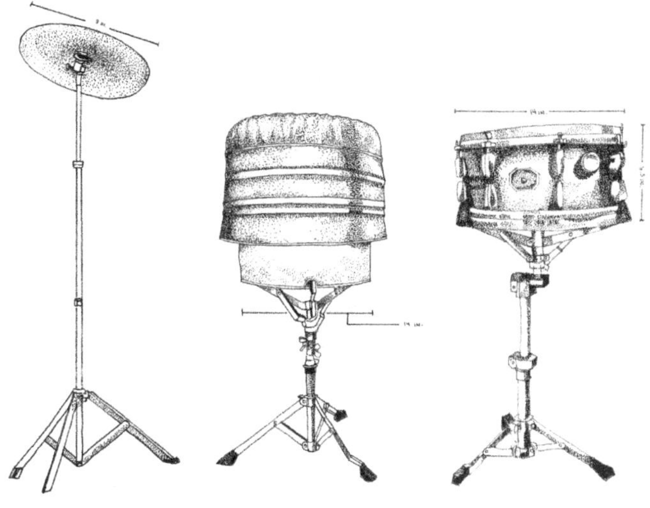

Violent Femmes sound aesthetic, but it also fits in well with the band's goal at the time to have a portable unit that would be easy to use while busking.

"We wanted to take this thing literally on the road," DeLorenzo says. "We wanted to be in the street, so I couldn't be hauling around a full drum set."

The drum set that DeLorenzo did eventually settle on, which he calls the "Femmes drum system," included the tranceaphone, a 6.5" × 14" Gretsch snare drum—the most conventional of DeLorenzo's instruments—and one nine-inch "no-name" cymbal.

"The cymbal was for accents," DeLorenzo says. "Not really for riding. I was using the tranceaphone like a ride cymbal. And it wasn't really that attractive or nice of a cymbal. It was just kind of something that you would hit out of … well, just because it was there and you got tired of hitting everything else."

While you can't see how odd this drum set looks while simply listening to *Violent Femmes*, one aspect of DeLorenzo's drumming that's unmistakable to the ear is the sound of his brushes. Traditionally used by drummers in jazz or country music, brushes are just what they sound like: metal fans that a drummer uses in place of drumsticks. They create a softer tone with less definition. Often used for low-volume ballads, brushes can also be swiped in patterns across a coated drumhead for a variety of signature "swishing" sounds. DeLorenzo used them almost unilaterally on *Violent Femmes*.

"My idea as a drummer in that trio was to present the unexpected and not only by standing up and playing such a ridiculous looking drum system," DeLorenzo says. "But also by playing brushes. I mean, who was playing brushes for a whole show at that particular time in musical history? Maybe if you were a jazz drummer or a country drummer, but certainly not rock and roll. Nobody was doing that."

So there it is: a snare drum, tranceaphone, and a weird little cymbal, all played with brushes—surely one of the most unusual drum sets in popular music history. Interestingly, though, it doesn't always sound that way. To a casual listener, in fact, DeLorenzo's drum set might even sound like a "regular" kit.

"What I tried to do just using a snare drum and the tranceaphone was *suggest* a drum set being played," DeLorenzo says, "even though there's not enough drums for it to be a drum set. But the way I divide up the beat between the tranceaphone and the snare drum, or sometimes how I divide up the left hand and the right hand on the snare drum, it kind of gives the feel as though it's almost some kind of a crippled drum set."

I remember discovering this trick on my own when I was a teenager and first put *Violent Femmes* on my headphones and tried to play along on my drum set. The first thing I didn't understand at the time was that the bass drum parts I thought I was supposed to be playing didn't exist. They were only notes implied by DeLorenzo's parts. And the eighth note ride patterns I was playing on the hi-hat—those notes were actually being played by DeLorenzo on the snare drum itself, or on the tranceaphone. Still, I managed to play along without too much trouble, inadvertently writing full drum set parts for ones that didn't exist. It was a bit of musical alchemy—or reverse alchemy, since I was turning gold into base materials—which DeLorenzo has heard before.

"It's always funny when I hear people cover Femmes material and they're playing a full drum set," DeLorenzo says. "It just doesn't sound right to me because it's not naked enough."

Perhaps the most famous example of this transposition is the Gnarls Barkey cover of "Gone Daddy Gone"—from their 2006 mega-smash, *St. Elsewhere*—on which a drum machine plays a straight-ahead full-on drum set part. And this is not to say that Gnarls Barkley was actually trying to recreate DeLorenzo's original part on their track—that's not how song reinterpretations work—but by using the drum pattern that DeLorenzo essentially did so much work to *avoid* playing (and which is basically the same beat a Casio would give you if you pressed the pre-programmed "rock beat" button), Gnarls Barkley makes clear just how much magic there is within DeLorenzo's original part.

"It's easy to have a full drum set to state the time and the rhythm," DeLorenzo says. "But when you have something that's fractured, like what I'm playing, it becomes a little bit more of an artistic endeavor."

Introducing limitations can serve as a catalyst for creativity in many art forms, and this was certainly the case with DeLorenzo's approach, because since he couldn't rely on changing drums or cymbals for different textures in different songs, he had to look elsewhere.

"I always wanted to devise some kind of a part that was different than just a standard two and four backbeat," he says. "So I really took some time and tried to arrange those percussion parts for those songs so that there would be some kind of variation."

Perhaps DeLorenzo's most notable technique to create such variation was his dramatic usage of dynamics—the shifting of volume from quiet to loud. For example, think of the breakdown on "Blister in the Sun," when the drums grow so quiet that the backbeat transforms into nothing more than the snapping of fingers. This drop in volume sets up the return of full-on drums in a way that generates explosive energy when they reappear, but not because the drums themselves are actually loud at that point—remember, they're still being played by brushes—rather simply because of the contrast in volume. It's a traditional device used by musicians throughout the ages, but one rarely employed by a drummer in a popular rock band.

"Most drummers think that to build excitement and tension, they need to get louder," says Ritchie. "But Victor is one of the only drummers who knows that you can also get quiet."

Such dynamics became a hallmark of the Violent Femmes' sound, and one unusual to the rock-and-roll landscape, in which most bands just max out at a volume and hold themselves there, as if letting their own arrangements run through a compressor, creating distinction between song sections simply by changing the number of notes or dropping instruments in and out. The Violent Femmes, on the other hand, learned early on that you can modulate the impact of a song through volume and touch.

"A lot of the rock music at that point in time was just full on, full off. Dynamics didn't really exist," DeLorenzo says. "But we were listening to jazz and country and folk music, and there's a lot of dynamics involved in those three different genres, so we brought that to the table and I incorporated that into the Femmes sound along with the idea of trying to play acoustic music in a hard rocking fashion. Which is what Jonathan Richman was doing, and Gene Vincent, to some extent. So we were just trying to carry on a little bit of those traditions that we knew about."

Such drumming choices affected not only DeLorenzo's drum parts but the songs as a whole, because in all those frequencies and spaces he left open with his "naked" drumming, other features of the songs were allowed room to operate in new and powerful ways.

"Victor was the opposite of bombastic," Ritchie says. "He was kind of a bombastic personality, but musically, he was quite subtle and understated, and with that, and with the acoustic bass and Gordon's acoustic guitar, well, guess what comes to the fore? The vocals."

Ritchie is emphatic that this instrumental approach to frame Gano's lyrics was a coordinated effort, and that the band—especially DeLorenzo—wrote their parts directly in conversation with Gano's lyrics.

"Victor's drum parts in particular," Ritchie says. "You could listen to the instruments without the lyrics and you'd hear him doing things that don't make sense. He's almost commenting on the lyrics with his drums."

"Certainly," DeLorenzo says. "I'm paying attention to what is being said and like any good actor on stage, you're reacting to what is going on around you. So that's certainly what is happening in regard to my drumming."

THE GUITAR

After all that, it's tempting to say that Gordon Gano's guitar work on *Violent Femmes* isn't nearly as unique as the drums or the bass, and while that might be true in the most obvious ways, Gano's approach is noteworthy for many reasons of its own, especially because of all the things he is not doing. Remember, this album was recorded in 1982. Gano was a fan of Johnny Thunders and the Ramones, and yet his guitar tone is more along the lines of Buddy Holly or "Sweet Jane"-era Lou Reed. The band would have been a different thing entirely if Gano had just been playing bar chords with distortion, and several tracks that are essentially punk at their core—like "Add It Up," "Prove My Love," or "Promise"—could have easily been played with a bigger, more distorted sound. Gano also avoided using effects that were popular at the time—no chorus, no delay—unlike contemporaries like The Police, U2, or The Cars. It's a choice that adds to the starkness and intimacy of the record and speaks to a type of sophisticated restraint perhaps rare to find in a nineteen-year-old. So while Ritchie and DeLorenzo rightly deserve the attention they get for their wild originality, had Gano approached his guitar tone and playing like most other rock guitarists of the time, *Violent Femmes* would've been foundationally different. It all starts with him.

Gano plays mostly rhythm guitar on the recordings, and he uses both an acoustic and an electric to do so. The acoustic was either a Takamine or an old Martin, depending on the track, and the electric was a 1969 sunburst Fender Telecaster

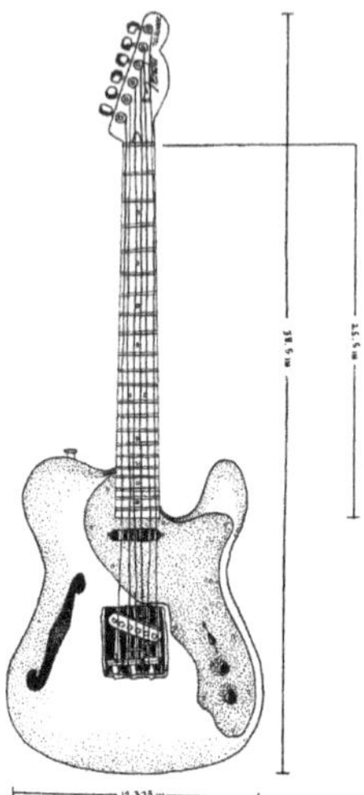

Thinline with an F-hole cutout. "Stained red," Gano says. "You could still see the wood grain."

Not long after the album was recorded, though, Gano got mugged and that Telecaster was stolen.

Luckily, he had a friend.

"It was a guy who was like, that's a shame you got mugged and you got your guitar stolen," Gano says. "And then he was like, you know, I know a lot of people around here, so let me just ask some questions and see if I can get your guitar back."

And Gano's friend did ask some questions. And he did get that guitar back.

"Amazing," Gano says.

But then the guitar got stolen again.

"And that time it was gone for good," Gano says. "It was on the road that it got stolen the second time, and I didn't have my contact anymore to say, 'I know some people around here, let me ask some questions.'"

Gano grows quiet.

"I toured with it a lot in the early days," he says, and then falls silent again. Finally, as if remembering a long-lost lover, he says, "What a great guitar."

3

The Studio

For sixteen years, it had been the Playboy Club. The lobby featured a sunken lounge. A ski chalet stood on the grounds. There were two golf courses and a building for employee housing that was known as the "Bunny Dorm." All the bunnies were gone by July 1982, though. Playboy had just sold the place.

But the recording studio was still open.

Castle Studios in Lake Geneva, Wisconsin, was an anomaly that had been installed in the main lodge of the Playboy Club as part of an effort to capitalize on the talent booked into the surrounding resort area, including its own cabaret. The list of stars coming through that venue had once included Frank Sinatra, Mel Tormé, and Sammy Davis Jr. The only talent on site in July of '82, though, was a trio of young men from Milwaukee with no record deal, a few guitars, and a metal bushel basket flipped over a floor tom.

"We made a deal with the studio," says Brian Ritchie. "They had a different rate for twenty-four-track and for eight-track. But they didn't actually have an eight-track recorder. So it's not like we could use the eight-track recorder. So what they did was, if we would agree to use only eight channels on the twenty-four-track two-inch tape, they would charge us the lower rate. So we did everything to eight-track. But it was on two-inch twenty-four-track tape."

It was a ridiculous arrangement, but the Violent Femmes had good reason to seek corners to cut. Remember, they were only in the studio because of a $10,000 loan from the father of their drummer, Victor DeLorenzo, and at a rate of roughly a thousand dollars a day, the pressure was on.

"There wasn't experimentation going on in the studio," says Gordon Gano. "Let's try recording it this way, now let's try a different arrangement or a different instrument … There was no time for that. We were just very focused on here's how we're going to go about it."

Part of the strategy was to choose which songs to record beforehand, a seemingly obvious step, but one that proved surprisingly difficult because of Gano's proclivity. Already he'd written so many songs that the band had enough to cover multiple albums' worth of material, including every track that would go on to appear on the band's first two albums. It was Ritchie who finally had what Gano calls "the brilliant idea" to pick only "the poppy songs" for the first album.

"Brian said, let's focus this album on being our rock songs and streamline it," Gano says, "and then have all of these other kinds of country and gospel and jazz—all these other kinds of influences that were in the songs that I had written and that we were playing—let's have those be on our second album." He chuckles at the hubris. "We have no record deal and we're already thinking in terms of what our second album will be like."

"The plan worked too well," Ritchie says. "People today are like, when are you going to put out another one like that again?"

With the songs selected, Van Hecke invited Gano to his apartment.

"I just sat there at my grand piano and I went through the songs note by note with him and edited them there," he says. Van Hecke even wrote Gano's songs out by hand, note by note on staff, so they could be copyrighted properly at the Library of Congress.

"Mark was a very good producer for us because he didn't want to expand our sound," Ritchie says, highlighting a key point for the band at the time, because with their pared down aesthetic and unorthodox instrumentation, the trio was often a magnet for suggestions about just how they could "improve"—recommendations that almost always leaned toward a more conventional approach. "Mark understood that our sound was unique and our approach was valid."

"He just threw himself into it completely," Gano says.

Tracking was live to two-inch tape, using an MCI tape machine and an MCI mixing board. DeLorenzo and Ritchie set up in the main tracking room within isolation booths built out of gobos dividers, while Gano was in a separate isolation room of his own, where he tracked guitar and lead vocals live.

By and large, the way in which Van Hecke approached recording the album, along with the band's use of mostly acoustic instruments, meant it basically could have been recorded in the same manner at any point during the preceding three decades or so.

"What I was going for were *The Sun Sessions* of Elvis," Van Hecke says.

"We recorded it pretty much exactly like what our live show was like," Ritchie says, "except we didn't go off on so many tangents, like we would do live. We'd stick to the song. But other than that, it was pretty much like our live show."

Van Hecke, a self-described microphone fanatic ("I wrote a treatise on them," he says) was pleased with the studio's selection. "I'm a Neumann nut," he says, of the German microphone company, whose classic U87 is what he used on Gano's vocals. Van Hecke put two room mics on the drums, spaced seven feet apart, and close-miked the snare drum and the tranceaphone, an instrument that Van Hecke didn't much care for. ("Victor thought it was a really cool invention," he says, "and I thought, it's an ash bucket, man.") By far the trickiest instrument to get right, Van Hecke says, was Ritchie's acoustic bass guitar.

"The drums weren't that much work," Van Hecke says. "But the bass was a ton of work."

Ritchie played the instrument aggressively, which is part of his unique sound and approach, but in the studio, Van Hecke says, "I had to ask him to modify it. He played with a lot of muscle, and it would overload the signal. I said, play lighter." He used three mics on the bass: a ribbon mic, another U87 over Ritchie's shoulder, and an SM57 in front, to capture the attack. "I wanted the percussion of the bass," Van Hecke says, "but I didn't want it to have so much buzzing because he was playing so hard."

Gano played acoustic guitar on four songs and his Fender Thinline Telecaster on the other six, running it through a Fender Deluxe Reverb that was closed off in another room and miked with an SM57.

The first engineer on the project was Glenn Lorbecki, who, Van Hecke says, "did not enjoy the project. He disliked the band, and two or three songs in, he wanted out. He quit and moved to Minneapolis." From there, John Tanner took over engineering duties. "We really hit it off," Van Hecke says. "John was very important in getting that album done." Together, he says that they "cheated like hell," cutting corners and working through the nights to save money.

DeLorenzo had the most recording experience of the group, Ritchie had some, and Gano was a total beginner, but because the band's approach was to basically just keep doing exactly what they'd been doing live, the recording went smoothly. "The thing we struggled with the most," Gano says, "were background vocals. Some things were really out of tune, and I mean, we weren't correcting anything. We were trying to get it the best we could. So yeah, the notes aren't perfectly in tune in a lot of places, but that's how it was. There's a liveness and a rawness to that problem. We wanted it to sound like we were playing right there in the speaker."

The majority of the backing vocals were handled by DeLorenzo, and if they needed someone with what DeLorenzo calls "a rousing, haranguing kind of a vocal," then Ritchie stepped in.

The studio itself presented a few mysteries as the days went by, especially in the first handful of sessions, while Lorbecki was still on the job.

"We'd tell Glenn what we wanted to do as far as the next song and the instrumentation," DeLorenzo says, "and he would start to set things up, but he would take a lot of time to kind of think about what he was doing and then we would come back for the next session, and we would notice, hey, in the rack over there, didn't there used to be a reverb there? Oh, ok. It's gone. All right. Then we come back next time. Wait a minute. Wasn't there a compressor there? What we found out was the studio was going into receivership. So they were selling all the equipment and they didn't tell us. They were just happy that they were getting money from us so they could pay the janitor to be our engineer."

And while there is some disagreement about whether or not Lorbecki was actually the studio's janitor as well as its engineer, what's clear is that the studio was basically falling apart around the band. Nonetheless, the resort was doing its best to maintain a façade of normalcy.

"One day, when we were recording 'Prove My Love,'" Ritchie says, "these chefs went riding by on a golf cart with their chef's hats on, and a whole baby pig with an apple in its mouth. They rode past our window and we just lost it. So that was an incomplete take."

Undeterred by suckling pigs or disappearing compression racks, the band forged ahead and finished recording in ten days. Van Hecke did the first mix himself, which Gano says, "probably sounded more correct to most people's ears," but the band felt it might have been missing a certain energy. "And so then we were like, no, we've got to be there," Gano says. "And that's how we all mixed it together."

4

The Songs

TRACK ONE: BLISTER IN THE SUN

It's the first song on the Violent Femmes' first album.

It's the first song most people mention when they think of the band.

At first, though, when Gordan Gano wrote it, "Blister in the Sun" wasn't even intended for the Violent Femmes.

"I'd gone to a poetry reading and met someone," Gano says, "a woman who I had exchanged numbers with, and she called to say that she was putting a band together, and she said it was going to be something like the Plasmatics."

Gano was interested. He was only sixteen or seventeen. Violent Femmes didn't exist yet—this was before he'd met DeLorenzo and Ritchie—and so he didn't have a band to play with. He did have dozens of songs that he'd already written, but still, on the night before the woman planned for her new group to meet, Gano started writing a new one.

"I wrote it thinking that it would be just something fun if I showed up and was like, well, I've got a song, if you're interested in a song that you could sing," he says.

The verses had a tight, almost hypnotic up and down melody, and the lyrics were unlike those of Gano's other songs, many of which were narrative to the point of dramatic monologue. This new song's lyrics were terse and inscrutable, compressed almost into haiku. Gano found himself mystified as to what they might mean.

"I don't know what's going on," he says. "Let me go on like a blister in the sun … What does that even mean? Why would anybody be excited about that?"

Something seemed to be working within the song's fabric, though. Gano could feel it.

"Maybe it captures something that you can't quite express," he says. "There's a feeling there that's, well, it doesn't make any sense in a normal way. But maybe there's some poetry involved, or some image, or some thought … "

As the song kept coming together, Gano endeavored to avoid cliché.

"I was trying to say something along the lines of 'I know you're the one,'" he says, of the chorus' closing lines, "and I thought, certain things have been used many times, like blue eyes, or the idea of some kind of beauty being the golden blonde. And there's the idea of being dainty and tiny, that's an aspect of beauty. So I thought, I wanted to have something that said something different or in a different way. And so I thought, well, how about big hands? Instead of your beautiful blue eyes, your dainty little hands … it's your big hands that I know that you're the one."

Gano finished the song that night but then the next day got a call telling him that the band meeting was canceled. He still had his new song, though, and later, when he teamed up with DeLorenzo and Ritchie, each musician added a new part to it that has since become an iconic phrase in the lexicon of American music.

"Brian said, hey, I think I have an intro for 'Blister,'" says DeLorenzo. "How about if I play this before the song starts? And he played that opening phrase, and I automatically just came up with those two stutter flams. It was almost like a reaction to what he was playing without even thinking."

The "stutter flams" DeLorenzo is referring to are the distinctive pair of two-note snare drum beats that he plays in answer to Ritchie's riff, and a flam is one of the traditional twenty-six rudiments for snare drum, played with two sticks hitting one note together, but with each stick striking the drum slightly apart, so that when they make contact, there's the smallest of spaces between hits. "I call them stutter flams because they're hitting a little bit off kilter," DeLorenzo says, "which gives it that strange little prodding feel to it."

"Victor DeLorenzo just doing something so unexpected like that … " says Gano, "that wouldn't be the normal thing that somebody might do at that point in the world of rock and pop music." Together, Ritchie's riff and DeLorenzo's drum response combine to form what he calls a fanfare. "That's why it was a great entrance number, starting a set or starting an album."

It's also why the phrase has been adopted by so many stadium organists and DJs at sporting events, where "Blister in the Sun"'s opening riff is played through public address systems across the globe for audiences who then respond by clapping DeLorenzo's stutter flams. To say it's an unexpected development in the life of the song would be a major understatement.

"I remember exactly the first time I heard it," DeLorenzo says. "I was in Milwaukee at the ballpark, and this was the day before 9/11, and I remember sitting in the stands with a good friend of mine who has since passed on, and we were just talking, and all of a sudden they played that intro over the public address system and we were both just shocked. I said, oh my god. This is crazy. How is the song getting everywhere like this?"

Today, there are even compilation albums of classic stadium sporting anthems and "Blister in the Sun" is right there along with the rest of them, between "Take Me Out to the Ball Game" and "Charge."

"It's incredible," Gano says. "But the other thing that I guess I wasn't expecting is that when this happens, the fans … nobody cares. It's just something else that is just sort of played and then drifts past everybody. But still, it's an incredible honor. I feel amazement. And I still do when I hear the Ramones' 'Hey, ho! Let's go' chant [at the ballpark]. Just to think of how they were, and how we were—it would not have been imaginable to be so much of a part of this aspect of mainstream society. I think that's great."

Before "Blister in the Sun" became an all-American call-and-response piece at major sporting events, though, it was simply the opening track on a new band's debut album, and the decision to place it there was an easy one.

"It really was a standout track," DeLorenzo says. "That's why we put it first on the record. It's almost like our calling card. It's like, this is what to expect, which is, I don't think you can expect anything when you listen to this record because it's not going to sound like a traditional record."

And while "Blister in the Sun" was never a single— "something that surprises a lot of people," Gano says—it is surely the most iconic of all tracks on this iconic album, and its slow-motion rise to cultural ubiquity reflects the band's unusual route to success as a whole. After all, a hit is simply a song that rises up the charts, with no suggestion of staying power. "Blister in the Sun," though? It has become an American classic, despite the fact that it never made a single appearance on the Billboard Hot 100 (although the magazine did recently name it #51 on its list of The 100 Best Pop Songs Never to Hit the Hot 100).

"We don't have hits," Ritchie likes to say, "we have classics," and when asked why "Blister in the Sun" has become such a classic, the band members have some ideas.

"It's just instantly recognizable because of how it starts with just the one instrument playing the melody," Gano says. "So it's right there. It's instant. And another thing that maybe works in its favor is its brevity and its simplicity."

"Probably because it's the most unique sounding," DeLorenzo says, "with the stops and with the use of dynamics."

"The easy sing-along chorus," Ritchie says, "and the lyrics—which can feel transgressive, even if they're not."

Ah yes. The lyrics. It's easy to see what Ritchie means by a suggestion of transgression. The chorus alone makes reference to being "so strung out" and "high as a kite." The verses have "stained sheets" that are rhymed with "my body beats." The meaning of it all, as Gano has said, remains somewhat mysterious even for him, but for listeners, the vacuum of literal meaning has sucked all types of implications into the void. Gano remembers well when one particularly popular reading of the song's lyrics was first brought to his attention.

"This was probably in the mid-1990s," he says, "so the record had been out for over ten years, and somebody said something about 'Blister in the Sun,' and what a fan they were. It was another musician. And they said something about what the song is about, without saying exactly what it was about. And I was like, 'Well, what's it about?' And they said, 'Well, everybody knows what it's about.' I said, 'I don't know. Why don't you tell me? What is it about?' And they're like, 'No, no, everybody … You wrote the song, and everybody knows what it's about.' I said, 'No, you gotta tell me.' They said, 'It's about masturbation.' And I said, 'I have never thought of that, and this is the first time I've even heard this.' And they were like, they were in total disbelief, because everybody they know is a fan, and everybody knows it's about masturbation, and I had never heard that, and I never thought of it. And I even remember one time telling that story with Brian Ritchie sitting beside me, and he's like, 'Well, what *is* it about, then?'" Gano laughs. "So I guess that's what he was thinking, too."

Gano doesn't mind people having their own interpretations.

"People sing along to it, and very often sing wrong words," he says, "so nobody really even knows what's being said in the song. I'm totally fine with that. The typical thing is, somebody will say, 'Let me go wild.' I've heard that many times. And it's not let me go wild. It's let me go *on*." The impenetrability of the song's meaning might even be part of its power, Gano suggests. "Maybe there's something of a mystique when you can't really follow the words exactly," he says. "I think of 'Louie Louie' and how nobody knew what was being sung in that song, and it was a huge hit."

Incredibly, the mystery around the lyrics of "Blister in the Sun" still often extends to the singer himself.

"I don't know if there's a specific word for this syndrome," Gano says, "but sometimes I look back at something I wrote, and instead of writing an 'A' I will write 'I,' or instead of 'I,' I'll write 'A,' and I always forget which way it is. It's to the point where I'd have to go back and find the original notebook with 'Blister in the Sun' written in it to see if I originally wrote it as *let me go on like I blister in the sun*, or, I think my original thought was, *let me go on like a blister in the sun*. They're almost interchangeable for me, though, and I like them both. Which way do you think it is?"

I'm stunned to have Gano turn the question on me. In truth, I had long been one of those who heard the chorus the wrong way, thinking it was "let me go wild" instead of "let me go on," but I don't mention that. Instead, I focus on the question at hand.

"Well," I say, "I mean, I hear 'a blister in the sun,' but 'I blister in the sun' sort of makes more literal sense … "

"Yeah," he says, "but I think I meant a blister like there's a blister, and then the sun will probably just keep blistering it more."

Parsing the meaning of "Blister in the Sun" with Gordon Gano is a situation I never expected to find myself in. I try to play it cool.

"Yeah," I say.

"I gotta talk to a doctor or a specialist," Gano says. "Maybe they'll say, yes, that's a classic syndrome. Like a form of dyslexia … "

I point out that not only is this lyrical dilemma of Gano's interesting on a personal level, but it's also fascinating because the line he's talking about is probably the most famous one he's ever written.

"It is, it is," he says. "You know, I get to a point right now … I'm thinking, how did I sing it last night?" He thinks for a second, then says, "Who knows."

As for the woman who invited him to form a new band with her so long ago, the one who inspired Gano to write "Blister in the Sun" in the first place, "I never saw her again, ever," he says. "Have no idea. Wouldn't remember her name. Even if you showed me a picture of her from back then I still wouldn't recognize it. But sometime after, some months later, I heard through somebody else that she had essentially disappeared and moved to Canada and joined a cult." He laughs. "She has no idea how narrowly she escaped."

TRACK TWO: KISS OFF

If you were to invent a device that could measure teen angst, like some Geiger counter for the soul, its needle might just shoot up and through the glass once it got in the vicinity of *Violent Femmes*. Track two, "Kiss Off," is as good place as any to start this conversation, because, well, just listen to the first lines.

"I need someone, a person to talk to / Someone who'd care to love / Could it be you / Could it be you?"

Here we go. Desire, isolation, a desperate search for love … All classics of the form. And what might come next? How about telling the whole world to fuck off? The song delivers. "You can all just kiss off into the air," Gordon Gano sings, as the chorus begins. "Behind my back, I can see them stare / They'll hurt me bad, but I won't mind / They'll hurt me bad, they do it all the time." You know the rest.

"You can't lose with a chorus like that," says Victor DeLorenzo, "especially when you've got a bunch of young teenagers singing it. They live through that song."

He's right, of course—those of us who felt Gano's lines at the time, we really really felt them—and as with so many emotional connections made through art, it's easy to then start to wonder: how much of this stuff is "true?" Like, is this guy singing about his own life, or is he just making it up?

"With a lot of the songs," Gano says, "there is a blend. It's just a blend of things I'm personally feeling, and then also fantasizing about and having just complete freedom to write anything that I feel. Maybe it's a kind of a character I'm imagining, but not any specific idea of who or what this character is. Some might be more autobiographical and some a little less. But usually there's some kind of a blend."

As for any suggestion that he might have been writing from the point of a view of a fictional character feeling "teen angst," though, Gano says that would not have happened. For one thing, he says, at the time he wrote the songs on *Violent Femmes*, he was still a teenager himself. "And I don't think that any teenager ever writes thinking, I will write something from the perspective of being a teenager." His lyrics were the real deal, basically, like a direct transmission, and that's probably why they've resonated so deeply for so long.

Gano also makes the point that desire and frustration— topics central to so many of the songs on *Violent Femmes*— are sentiments felt by humans of all ages. He singles out the idea of sexual frustration as a key component of the potent emotional cocktail known as "teen angst," but when asked about the relevance of still singing songs written by a teenager today, Gano likes to respond with a question.

"Does sexual frustration end for everybody?" he says. "Once you turn twenty, or once you're even in middle age? Is there nobody middle-aged who doesn't feel sexual frustration? Obviously the answer is that there is this incredible amount of sexual frustration, in differing degrees, for the entire world. It doesn't stop as a teenager. When writing, I never thought I'm writing teenage songs. I'm writing songs."

Gano finds it easy to connect to the songs he wrote as a teenager, not because he's found a way to emotionally travel back in time, but rather because he feels the songs are strong enough to apply to all stages of life. "I would have a problem with a song that I thought was not a good song," he says, "and there's some little places here and there where I think, oh, that could have been maybe a little better, you know. And if there's a song that makes me cringe or squirm, then, you know, we're not doing it. But there isn't anything like that on the first album."

He thinks for a moment about the show he played the night before.

"When I sing these songs," he says, "I never think about what I thought or what I was like when I wrote it when I was fifteen, sixteen, or seventeen. Or almost never. I mean, it's there. But I'm not thinking about that. Last night I sang all these songs. I sang these songs so many times that there's never this gap between how I am now and how I was then as a person, as a writer, as a singer. There's just a musician in Violent Femmes."

Still, if there's one line on this album that seems tailored most exclusively for an existentially troubled teenager, it might be the classic threat that starts the song's second verse: "I hope you know that this will go down on your permanent record." The terror and ridiculousness held within those thirteen words are so potent and sharp that you can almost smell the rank gym clothes and musty chalk dust rising around them.

"Personally, I think of that as one of the lesser lines of the song," Gano says. "That is the non-essential part of the song, in a way. But then I have heard people over the years say how much that resonated, not just with them, but with people they knew, and that it was a really big deal. And I just thought, wow, this." He laughs, recalling the specific inspiration for the phrase as somewhat vague. "It was a period in time where that was a thing that teachers would say, and I guess it was supposed to improve behavior: 'You better watch out or else this will go down on your permanent record.' I definitely heard that, not as much directed at me personally, although it might have been at some point … I'm sure it would have had to have been at some point."

The torment evoked in the line, as well as the emotional turmoil roiling throughout all of the lyrics in "Kiss Off," is echoed in the song's dynamic instrumental arrangement. Opening with Gano's voice and an acoustic guitar, the first verse is a quiet and restrained affair, setting up the chorus—in which the whole band appears—to feel like an explosion.

"The structure of this song is incredible," DeLorenzo says. "When Brian comes in with that fill and the band falls in, it's so dramatic and so powerful."

Perhaps the most explosive part of "Kiss Off," though, is the wildly unhinged instrumental section after the second verse, which the band improvised live.

"All the improvisation is true improvisation," DeLorenzo says. "When we played live, of course, things could go on for a while longer, but we knew we had to keep things pretty tight in the recording just because at that time, there were no CDs, so you had to figure you only had about sixteen minutes per side on a vinyl album. So we had to keep things tight."

Wild improvisation and threats from imaginary teachers aside, the bridge of "Kiss Off" is surely the song's most defining feature. A lyrical countdown from one to ten, listing all of the sources of emotional torment for the narrator—*one cause you left me, two for my family, three for my heartache, four for my headaches, five for my lonely, six for my sorrow*, and so on—it's a thirty-one-second interval of despair that has secured a place in pop culture infamy. When Gano reaches number eight on the list, though, the intense emotional conflict he's been singing about gets relieved for just a moment by a stroke of sharp cutting humor. "Eight, eight … I forget what eight was for," he sings, nailing the moment so well that Penn Jillette of Penn and Teller, of all people, once made it a point to explain to Gano just why the line works so well.

"He told me he was a fan, and then he got very specific," Gano says. "'Kiss Off,' he said, 'when you say number eight, I forget what eight was for?' He said, 'That is great comedic timing.' He said, 'If it came earlier it wouldn't work, and if it came later, it wouldn't work. Number eight was the exact spot it needed to be. Number eight. That is the spot. That is where you need to put it. And you did it. So good job.'"

Gano has found that his humor can sometimes be lost on people, though.

"I do get asked occasionally, 'Do you always forget what eight was for?'" he says. "And I'm like, Well, I … that's how I wrote it." He laughs, but then adds that a lapse in memory might have been part of his initial inspiration. "It could have been that I had it in my head, and then when I was writing it down, I got to eight, and I was like, oh, what was that one? And then I thought, well, I forget what eight was for, and I thought, Oh, that's good! I like that. That's better than whatever it was. That's very likely, I think, how I might have first written it."

TRACK THREE: PLEASE DO NOT GO

Gordan Gano was being driven to Canada. He had a show there that night and a few hours to kill. I was lucky to have him on the phone with me. He doesn't know me. He was just helping me out. The world whooshed past on the other end of the line as I sat at my desk, considering just how I was going to ask my next question. I was thinking about the song "Please Do Not Go," *Violent Femmes'* third track, and how it sounds a little bit like a reggae song. I didn't want to ask Gano if he had tried and failed to write a reggae song, though, so instead, I said, "Were you listening to a lot of Bob Marley when you wrote 'Please Do Not Go?'"

"Ding, ding, ding, ding, ding!" he said.

And that made me feel better.

"I was listening to *a lot* of Bob Marley," he said. "But I guess, thankfully for me and maybe for everybody, when that comes out it doesn't sound much like Bob Marley."

Gano is right—"Please Do Not Go" does not sound like Bob Marley—or Jimmy Cliff, for that matter, who Gano says he was also listening to a lot at the time, after falling in love with the soundtrack to the reggae-infused Jamaican crime film *The Harder They Come.* You can hear a touch of their influence, though. That hidden one-drop—the invisible emphasis on the three—that gives the song its effervescent uplift. The way Gano just barely says "mon" instead of "man" in the first line. The rhythm guitar emphasizing the offbeat.

"I probably even told Brian and Victor, this is a reggae song," Gano said, "and it just fell on deaf ears for them as a rhythm section. Either they couldn't do it, or didn't know how, or thought, that's a terrible idea and we refuse to do that. It's probably a combination of all those things, to give them credit."

Gano thought about it all for a second. More of the country whooshed past.

"Brian Ritchie can play seemingly anything and sound great," he said, as if rethinking the song's genesis. "Except I don't know if it's that he can't play reggae, or he just refuses and doesn't want to, or some combination … "

Later I asked Ritchie about it. His response was, "We're a terrible reggae band."

I didn't press. It's an answer that seemed like enough, because it speaks more to the soul of Violent Femmes and less to their technical prowess (especially since, as Gano pointed out, Ritchie could surely have been an excellent bassist in a reggae band if he wanted to be). In fact, the song's most noteworthy instrumental moment is yet another of this album's testaments to Ritchie's technical skill: the eight bar bass solo that follows the second chorus, at which point all other instruments have stopped playing at all.

"It might be the longest unaccompanied bass solo on any popular recording," Ritchie says.

And yet it's so melodic and hooky that I think many people don't even know it's a bass solo. Even Gano says the strangeness of the part was largely lost on him at the time.

"I didn't have as strong of a sense of how unusual it was," he says, "because it just sounded so good and felt right."

Perhaps for Ritchie and DeLorenzo, it was important to ignore Gano's original reggae inspiration in an effort to keep the song true to the band and not an attempt to be something that they weren't.

"Victor called it our comedy song," Gano said. "Or something like that. And I was like, oh, I'd never heard that, but he definitely makes some funny sounds and choices for some of his background vocals in the *bye bye* part. And it's like, well, he was just trying to go further in that direction, to say that this can't be taken too seriously, and it shouldn't, so let's try to make it work and just make it a funny song." Again there was a pause on the line. Again more whooshing. "Yeah, but I never thought of it as funny," Gano said. "I always thought of it as kind of pleasant."

TRACK FOUR: ADD IT UP

I was never disallowed music. As a child, I had whatever albums I wanted—Dead Milkmen, Misfits, Suicidal Tendencies, Dead Kennedys … Lyrical content was never an issue. I can't recall once being told that something was too loud or inappropriate. Still, whenever it came on my stereo, "Add It Up" was the one song I would always turn down. It just felt too dangerous.

"That's great," Gano says. "It should feel like that."

I guess the risk was really in the song's first three verses, the ones structured around an escalating sequence of sexual desires, each starting with a potent new question: "why can't I get just one kiss?" building to "why can't I get just one screw?" and culminating with the final—and shocking (to a fourteen-year-old)—"Why can't I get just one fuck?"

"It probably still has some impact," Gano says. "But culturally, things were different back then. I think somebody who didn't have that experience from years ago … I don't think they could really get a sense of how explosive it felt, or how there was a feeling of something perhaps even a little dangerous in it."

The danger, and it was dangerous, was the feeling that our own secrets were being revealed by Gano, and amid the intimacy of the band's acoustic arrangement, his exposed voice just felt so keenly like it was a soul being bared. Like it was *our* soul being bared.

"Years ago, somebody told me that when they heard this album, they had this strange feeling," Gano says. "They felt like they were invading somebody's privacy. They felt like they were reading somebody's private diary."

It's the exact type of intimacy writers so often strive for, but for Gano, he says any connection between a listener and his material is a link made only with his art, not to him as a person.

"If somebody knows, and many people do, every single word on the first album," he says, "I don't feel any invasion of privacy, I don't. But I go further. I don't think that that person knows me at all." As a songwriter, Gano says he's able to make expressions of vulnerability without feeling vulnerable at all. "I feel like I can express anything," he says, "and it doesn't feel like I'm saying too much."

He credits his parents with this ability to separate himself so completely from a performance.

"They were both in theater," Gano says, remembering times when, from a distance, he might hear his parents arguing in the house only to realize, with great relief, that they were just running lines for a show. "I think that that's a big part of everything, that I grew up with the concept of stage and a performance and of taking on characters."

Theater was an insulating force for DeLorenzo too, who says that the idea of playing songs like "Add It Up," which to many people might have seemed emotionally revealing or shocking, was never much of an issue for him.

"Well, I was coming from Theatre X, where I had already been on stage naked," DeLorenzo says. "So to me, to present myself with clothes on and just listen to someone sing something that's a little bit controversial, I didn't feel any pressure or any oddness or embarrassment. I had already had myself literally and figuratively stripped down enough because of my work in theater. So listening to something like this was, it was pretty tame, to tell you the truth."

The way Gano remembers it, Brian Ritchie did have a problem with "Add It Up," though, but it had nothing to do with the lyrics. When Ritchie first heard the song, "He said, let's not do this one," Gano says. At the time, Gano had so many songs written inside of what DeLorenzo calls his "magic notebook" that if someone didn't like one, he would just think, no big deal. I have a bunch more. In this case, though, Gano dug in.

"I was like, this is one of the best ones—maybe the best— because of its intensity and the feeling of it," he says. He asked Ritchie what the problem was. "And Brian said, 'It's boring.' I said, 'What? To me, it's one of the most exciting.' And then I said, 'Well, why do you think this song is boring?' And he said, 'Only two chords ... the same two chords, back and forth the entire song.'"

Only two chords. Ritchie was right, the song does only have two chords, but Gano was confident the song's worth had nothing to do with its harmonic complexity, or lack thereof. He held his ground. "And then later," Gano says, "Brian said that [the song's limited chord structure] forced him and Victor to keep playing variations in their rhythmic accompaniment. And so it's actually worked to the betterment of the song and the recording, because all those shifts and changes are great. It wouldn't be as exciting without them."

"Well, that song is like twenty minutes long and it only has two chords," Ritchie says. "But the arrangement is amazing.

There is a lot going on with the rhythm section. A lot of different feels."

There's the dramatic a capella introduction, the hard-driving first three verses, the wild bass solo between them, the straight-ahead chorus, the broken down third and fourth verses (divided by the rare Gano guitar solo), and then the final chorus ending with its bold melodic statement on bass. It's a dynamic rollercoaster ride.

"It was our job to arrange things," DeLorenzo says, "and being the musicians that we are, we damn sure wanted to make sure that the songs were different from one another."

One section that really stands out is the fourth verse, where Gano starts repeating the phrase "mo-my-mama mama-mo-my-mum" in such a rapid delivery that it borders on rap.

"I'm guessing that was inspiration from Blondie," Gano says, "because I hadn't heard any rap except from Blondie at that point." The Trashmen's 1963 song "Surfin' Bird"—with its classic "everybody's heard about the bird" line—might have also been an inspiration, he says. But the repeated references to "momma" in this part of the song—followed by the verse in which Gano sings, "Broken-down kitchen at the top of the stairs / Can I mix in with your affairs? / Share a smoke, make a joke"—brought with it an unexpected complication.

"One review singled out that song," Gano says. "It was one of the first things ever written about us. It said that the song 'Add It Up' is a song about Gordon Gano smoking pot with his mom. And my mom was not happy about that. She was not happy. But she knew that couldn't be what the song was about, because that never happened. And then

Brian Ritchie, at some point, very dryly told me, like, well, you know everybody knows that if it's like a blues song, or a Bob Dylan thing, and you're saying mama like about your girl, you spell it MAMA. You don't spell it MOMMA. That's Mom. You spelled it the wrong way. And I'm like, really. Oh, I guess I think maybe you're right."

TRACK FIVE: CONFESSIONS

Imagine you're seated in an old, darkened theater. The curtains are just starting to part. First you see one actor, then two, and then more and more until there's a whole chorus on stage. They all start snapping their fingers. "People, what are they worrying about today?" they sing. "The people worry, what are they worrying about today?" And now a new character steps into the light. "What are they worrying about today?" he says. "News headlines!"

This isn't a real musical I'm describing, of course. It's just the imaginary one Gordon Gano had in mind when he wrote "Confessions," back when he was picturing the song as an upbeat show tune.

"That's where it came from," he says. "And then I slowed it down and put the minor chord in the riff with it, which changes the whole idea musically and rhythmically. But it's still there."

Gano's parents were in theater. His bandmate, Victor DeLorenzo, worked in theater. The idea of performative storytelling was all around Gano as a young artist, and so it makes sense that he would work in this vein. And Gano has written for the stage many times since, including scoring a whole musical in 2023—"Run Bambi Run," the story of Lawrencia "Bambi" Bembenek, a former Milwaukee police officer who was convicted of murder and then escaped from prison. Even if you didn't know about the song's theatrical roots, though, just a cursory listen to "Confessions" reveals the drama at hand. Opening quietly and somberly, the song goes on to unspool a five-minute-and-thirty-three-second monologue of sorts about a man cracking up under the pressures of loneliness. "I'm so lonely," Gano sings in the second verse, capturing the song's general vibe, "feel like I'm gonna crawl away and die." Gano plays electric guitar on the track and DeLorenzo uses a full drum set, even switching from brushes to drumsticks once the band launches into the explosive instrumental section after the third verse.

"The lyrics were building to that point," Ritchie says, of the logic behind the instrumental shift, and the band's responsiveness to Gano's lyrics continues throughout the song, eventually reaching an apocalyptic jazz-influenced freakout after Gano sings about wanting to "hack it apart" in the final verse.

According to Gano, the ability of the band to reflect his lyrical content with such deft instrumental dexterity is largely a credit to the jazz background of Ritchie and DeLorenzo.

"They knew so much more about jazz," Gano says. "I was late coming to jazz, and I love jazz, but at the time of recording the first album, if ever they were doing something that was getting more syncopated or jazzy or contrasting, it was just flowing by me. I couldn't have possibly even followed it all in my head. I was just trusting them, thinking, I know that it sounds good. I've just got to keep delivering on my end."

Gano did deliver on his end, of course—he was the songwriter, after all—and while he might not have provided the same technical fireworks as his bandmates, he made his own contributions, especially in how he managed to write "Confessions" in a way that matched the despondent mood of the lyrics to its opening minor chord and yet managed to maintain the feeling even after it shifted to a major.

"One time somebody said, when you hit that major chord, it's still so sad. Desolate. And yet you're playing a major chord," Gano says. "They said that's when I knew that you were good, to be able to choose to do that and to pull it off. But I hadn't thought it through like that. I just wrote it like that and felt it and felt that's what I want to do."

Gano says that he knew so little about any of the so-called rules of songwriting—lyrically, and especially musically— that when he was writing the songs on the first album, he made many choices like this that others found perplexing. Gano didn't know they were unusual at all, though, and to him, this was an asset.

"I didn't feel any constraints by whatever the rules were," he says. "I didn't know them, so I could just write."

It's an artistic freedom that applies to the whole album, Gano says, adding that even if the young trio didn't "know better," what was more important was that they didn't care.

"There's a certain energy of youth that comes across," he says. "It's the punk thing of being inexperienced and or technically not proficient, but it's actually no hindrance. It's even something to have a swagger about."

TRACK SIX: PROVE MY LOVE

It's easy to forget that not too long ago, musicians really had to consider how they sequenced an album. Side one, side two: each required its own logic. It was like every record had two mini albums within it, each needing its own opener and closer and an arc between the two that made sense. *Violent Femmes* is a perfect example. "Blister in the Sun" is custom-made to be an album opener, "Confessions," with its slow build and dramatic conclusion, is an impeccable closer for side one, and then once the record (or cassette) is flipped, the listener is launched into side two with "Prove My Love," blasting off like a little snare drum-powered rocket.

"We call that the Femmes beat," Victor DeLorenzo says, of the song's iconic opening snare pattern. "I think it was probably a case of, OK, let's have a song that starts with the drums. And then I said, OK, how about this? And now whenever I play it, people know right away that that's 'Prove My Love.'"

DeLorenzo's boom-taptap boom-tap instantly conjures a certain early-era rock & roll uplift, hard-driving yet poppy and bright, but when Gano first wrote the song, he had a different direction in mind.

"I was thinking of it like a Johnny Thunders kind of thing," Gano says, referring to the former New York Dolls guitarist, whose band the Heartbreakers Gano saw when he was fifteen and visiting his brother in New York City. And while it's not impossible to imagine "Prove My Love" being performed by a band in the vein of Johnny Thunders and the

Heartbreakers, the song as we know it today ended up being shaped by less bombastic influences.

"Gene Vincent and the Blue Caps," Gano says, citing one of the Violent Femmes' primary inspirations, an early rockabilly act whose influence you can hear throughout the album. "That was an inspiration, something that we all really liked a lot. I think all three of us. Sometimes I forget how, when I first heard that music … There's something really riveting and really grabbing about it. Still is."

Another influence that seems to have been lifted right off of an oldies station is Gano's line "third verse, same as the first," which he sings (obviously, I suppose) at the start of the song's third verse. It's a line adapted from Herman's Hermits' 1965 mega hit, "I'm Henry the VIII, I Am," in which they sing "second verse, same as the first." For Gano, though, he wasn't quoting Herman's Hermits at all.

"I hadn't even thought of that," he says. "I don't think I'd heard it, or if I'd heard it, I didn't remember it. I just knew very well the Ramones way." He's talking about the Ramones' song "Judy is a Punk," off their 1976 debut *Ramones*, in which they lift the Herman's Hermits line and sing it before their own second verse. "I loved it from the Ramones," Gano says, "and I love the Ramones, so I just dropped it in at some point, probably playing it live. I didn't write the song with that there, but probably very early on I thought, I'll do the first verse again rather than try to write another one, and just, you know, say that beforehand."

For Gano, this chain of influence from Herman's Hermits to the Ramones to Violent Femmes is an apt one to trace the lineage of so much of what the Violent Femmes were trying to do as a band.

"We were just drawing on this older rock-and-roll and then doing it through this punky kind of way," Gano says. "So I think it's probably true that [the song is] all of that, that it comes from that kind of punk thing, but then also definitely relates to the earlier fifties music, for sure."

Instrumentally, "Prove My Love" is a good example of what Ritchie means when he describes his role in Violent Femmes as not only playing bass, but "filling in for the bass drum." In the stripped-down intro and verses of the song, in which Gano either sits out on the guitar or is just striking a muted chord on the downbeat with DeLorenzo, there is a huge gap around the one and three of the measures, in which you can hear Ritchie simulating a traditional bass drum pattern on his Ernie Ball Earthwood acoustic bass guitar. Interestingly, because the other instruments have left so much sonic room for Ritchie to work with in those spots, the instrument sounds in many ways even more powerful and punchy than it might have if it had otherwise been accompanied by a bass drum.

On most of the album, Ritchie handles the solos, but here Gano takes one for himself after the second chorus. He's playing an electric guitar on the recording, but his approach—which is mostly just a rhythmic pattern of chords—was one that he developed while busking on an acoustic.

"If we were playing on the street and I went to a guitar solo to hit single notes, they wouldn't be heard because I was just playing an acoustic guitar," he says. "So I was trying to make it as loud as I could, and that's what developed the rhythm acoustic guitar solo there."

It's also why Ritchie and DeLorenzo barely play at all in the section, digging in with a type of inverted stop time, in which they accent the two and four of each measure and nothing else.

"They're playing so minimally," Gano says. "And then it's just the space is there for the guitar. Maybe at first I started trying to play some notes with it and then realized, what if I just do some other rhythm and try to hit mostly full chords and do these shifts and these rhythms that would be able to be heard playing on the street."

It's a stylistic interplay that speaks to the countless hours the Violent Femmes spent busking before the record was made. Together, the three musicians often sound more like one instrument on this album than a band of them, as if they were a three-piece sonic jigsaw puzzle able to change respective shapes to fit together in whatever configuration each song required.

Thinking of the variety of influences that came together on this track, Gano starts mulling the lyrics. "Well, I got a question for you," he says. "Does Baskin-Robbins still have 31 flavors?"

"I don't know," I say. I try to remember the last time I saw one around, let alone went to one. "Do they exist? I don't even know."

Together we consider the passage of time, and perhaps the taste of ice cream.

"Special favors come in 31 flavors … " Gano says, quoting himself from the song's second verse. "Yeah, there we go, pass the Lifesavers. Well, Lifesavers still exist. I presume."

TRACK SEVEN: PROMISE

"Now we're hitting probably the two songs that might not be considered the classics, or the ones that maybe are not as beloved," Gordan Gano says, and an involuntary grunt comes out of my face. It's a grunt of shock. Gano is talking about tracks seven and eight on *Violent Femmes*—"Promise" and "To the Kill"—and it's surprising for me to even think of them as individual songs, let alone ones that might be less beloved than others, because to me, *Violent Femmes* isn't a collection of different tracks—it's really just one continuous statement. I assume you either love the whole album or just haven't heard it yet. There's no in between. Not that I don't believe Gano about these songs being less popular. Of course, some parts of any album are surely more treasured than others. But the real surprise for me is the way in which Gano has just raised a curtain, revealing to me my own bias. It's actually sort of embarrassing. I'm a writer here. I'm supposed to be impartial. When it comes down to it, though, I'm still just a fan. That eleven-year-old who imprinted on the album back in 1988 isn't so easy to shake.

As if sensing all of this going through my head, Gano says, "'Promise' is pretty popular. It rocks strong." It's like he's stepped back from his previous position simply out of consideration for my feelings.

I don't need his sympathy. I assume a critical position. I ask myself, yeah, why would "Promise" be less of a favorite for someone? The structure is unusual, for one thing.

"Does this song even have a chorus?" I say.

"No," he says, "but it has, well, it has a *tagline*: 'and your unhappiness is only a guess.'"

For sure that's a catchy line, and it's repeated a couple times, so it is *like* a chorus, but it only lasts a few seconds. And then there's the strange way Gano sings the word "unhappiness."

"I sing 'And you're unhappi ... '—stop!—' ... ness is only a guess,'" Gano says, parsing his unusual phrasing. "So I think a lot of people, maybe even a majority, hear it as 'You're unhappy. This is only a guess.' I just break it up in that bizarre way."

I mention the missing chorus to Victor DeLorenzo, and while he concedes that it might not have one, "for a song without a chorus," he says, "it's got such hooky parts. I mean, the bridge part with the vocal thing there ... "

Ah yes. The bridge with the vocal thing there. The da-da-da-da-da part. It's such an incredible ear worm that just thinking about it gets it stuck in my head, and then when I go into my kitchen later and see my wife doing the dishes, I sneak up behind her and sing those first five notes, very quietly, into one ear and then at once she starts singing the rest. It's like I've triggered a chain reaction, one that keeps going all evening, with both of us singing until bed.

"What I always loved was when it would get to a part where Gordon would start to rap a little bit," DeLorenzo says, talking about the first half of the bridge, before the da-da part, "and then I would just dig into the snare drum and do what you would consider to be more of a standard jazz brush part, where I would just be swishing a lot and still holding time, but the time isn't being marked, it's kind of floating. So then when I go back to the beat, it really digs in and it gives it a nice propulsion."

This is classic DeLorenzo. Playing with dynamics, utilizing jazz tricks within the framework of pop. And as Gano said, "Promise" does indeed "rock hard," especially on that bridge section where DeLorenzo comes out of his swishing. The song might be the most straight-ahead rocker on the whole album, in fact, a tone that Gano establishes right away with his aggressive guitar introduction played on the electric.

"There is something about the chords I was writing with that is kind of unusual," Gano says. "They're changing so fast. And then they go through a progression, and it's just kind of crazy, but it has its own sense to it. When I was writing it, I wouldn't have known that this was unusual musically." It's a progression that Ritchie makes note of as well, saying that in recent years, he's noticed it bears a striking resemblance to the White Stripes' "Seven Nations Army."

Gano's theatrical inclinations are at work once again in "Promise," most evidently on the chorus where he attaches a stutter to the narrator. It's the perfect affect for this outsider protagonist, a classic Gano invention, who, after asking if someone might ever want him to care, adds, "Disregard my nervousness / Ple-please ignore my vacant stares." At one point in the song's life, Gano says his lyrical experimentation ranged even further. "There's a section of 'Promise' where I used to try to go into some kind of poetry," he says, "and it was absolutely inspired by Patti Smith, who I was, and am, a huge fan of. Yet it wasn't anything close to as good as where she's at. It was just sort of like wanting to be like that, and I would do it live, and then, sometime before we recorded,

I realized, I don't think this is that good. I've got to cut it out. And so we cut it out before we recorded, and I'm so glad, because it was just my being a Patti Smith wannabe, ranting on some little theme or idea, and then bringing it back to the song, like she does on *Horses*. I'm very glad that even at that age I decided that I was going to cut that out."

He thinks about the section for a moment, remembering just what it was that he used to sing there.

"I think you'd agree," he says, as he listens to the inside of his head. "You know what? There's no question you would agree. I'm convinced. It's starting to play in my head right now, and there's no way … No, no way."

TRACK EIGHT: TO THE KILL

Back when Gordon Gano was still a teenager and writing the songs that would go on to appear on *Violent Femmes*, he liked to go to a disco club in Milwaukee.

"This is like my version of Cinderella," he says, "because the last bus that would take me home left at midnight. And I didn't have any money to take anything other than the bus, so I had to make sure I was out of the disco by midnight to get back home."

Gano had heard that the disco was having a talent show one night and decided to go. He had a new song that he thought might be a winner.

"I thought it was kind of a dance song," he says. "It was 'To the Kill.'"

Let's be clear here. "To the Kill" is not a dance song. "To the Kill" a slowish meander through the mind of a man whose girlfriend has taken all of his money and moved to Chicago, leaving him behind with nothing but pain. It's punctuated by moments of freakout free jazz improvisation. And while I guess someone could find a way to dance to it if they so desired, the song is essentially the opposite of disco.

Still, Gano went to the disco that night and played it.

"So I play 'To the Kill' at the disco with just me and my guitar," Gano says. "By the way, people always looked at me there like, what are you doing here? Yeah, I didn't fit in at all. And anyway, I got second place. I got a second-place prize."

"Who won?" I say.

"I don't remember. I'm sure it was a karaoke kind of thing."

There was no glass slipper for Gano that night, though he did catch his bus home by midnight. And don't forget the second place prize. All in all a success, I'd say. And maybe "To the Kill" did sound more like a dance song back then. Songs evolve over time. It's hard to gauge exactly what it might have sounded like inside of that club on that night, but one thing that's certain is that the song didn't yet feature the improvised eight-measure instrumental introduction that it has on the recording.

"That would have been the idea of either Brian or Victor," Gano says, "or both of them, because there's no way I could have come up with that."

"Gordon would just hold on for dear life when we went off into advanced improvising," Ritchie says.

"I probably had sweat popping out on my forehead," Gano says, "trying to just keep counting and ignore what they were doing and make a little noise myself. I remember hanging on by my fingernails on that one."

Though it wasn't part of Gano's initial vision for the song, that improvised section—and all the other moments like it that appear on the album—became vital to the band's identity.

"If we didn't have those improvised sections," Ritchie says. "It'd just be … folk music."

And while I'm not sure that's exactly the case, even if "To the Kill" does sound more like folk music than disco, another aspect of the song that surely keeps the track from sounding too folksy is the fact that both Gano and Ritchie play electric guitar and bass on the track, respectively.

"That was for the toggle switch," Ritchie says, of his choice to use an electric, referring to the tiny lever on the instrument that shifts between pickups, a tool that Ritchie utilized to dramatic effect on the intro, playing it like an instrument of its own, toggling back and forth in a rapid series of triplets at one point to create a type of hook. I can sing the toggle switch part right now, without even hearing the track.

These days, when they play the song live, the introduction that once induced such panic in Gano is one of his favorite parts. "I just love it," he says, "because I'm not sure exactly what's going to happen. And now I relax with it thoroughly and enjoy it." Another difference between the recording and the live version today is a small change that Gano recently made to the lyrics. "I'm tired of saying bitch," he says. "This bitch took my money and went to Chicago. I got tired of saying that recently, so I changed it, and I really like it. I say, 'Mitch took … ' and I don't know if anybody notices. I try to say it as clearly as I can. *Mitch* took my money and he went to Chicago, and I think that's hysterically funny. I love saying that every night, and I'm thinking, is anybody hearing? I'm trying to say Mitch as clearly as I can." He laughs. As for that original lyric, though, the one about a woman taking all the narrator's money and moving to Chicago? Well, Gano says, he has a small confession to make.

"That part's actually true," he says. "That happened literally. I didn't have much money, but it's all I had."

"How much did she take?" I say.

"Hey. You're getting personal now."

TRACK NINE: GONE DADDY GONE

Back in the days when the Violent Femmes were still busking on Milwaukee street corners, Brian Ritchie noticed something unusual about the people who'd stop to listen.

"We realized that when we would play with Victor, people would give us less money," he says. "It was because he was older and more put-together looking." So sometimes Ritchie and Gano would play without DeLorenzo, in hopes of getting more tips. "We were playing as a duo like that one night," he says, "and Gordon had this song, 'Gone Daddy Gone.' It's in D minor, which means that you can just use all of the white keys on a piano. Or a xylophone. And I had this xylophone … "

Let's pause here to consider the business plan. A band decides to sneak out without their drummer, in hopes of looking younger and more destitute—so as to draw more donations—and then the bassist decides, wait, today I won't play bass. I'll play … xylophone. It's a risky marketing strategy, to say the least.

"The xylophone was because I was influenced by Brian Jones and the Stones and the work he had done with xylophone and mallets on the Stones recordings," Ritchie says, leaving out one important fact. "Brian didn't play xylophone," Gano says. "But his attitude is like, I can make it work. He probably thought a xylophone would sound good on this, and then I think he found one on the street somewhere, and then he thought, well let me just teach myself how to play this and then come up with a part and play it."

Ritchie has done this with other instruments. Gano specifically remembers the time when the band was on tour in Australia and Ritchie decided he wanted to learn how to play the didgeridoo, an instrument notoriously difficult to master because of the required technique known as circular breathing. "He taught himself that in about two days," Gano says.

In any case, the xylophone part Ritchie worked up for "Gone Daddy Gone" on the street that day in Milwaukee worked well in the song, and regardless of whether it garnered more tips for the band or not, it became an integral layer of the song's arrangement. When it came time to record, though, the part presented a problem. The band was tracking live, but Ritchie couldn't play xylophone and bass at the same time.

"So that's the song we went into recording thinking we're going to do some overdubs," Gano says.

"'Gone Daddy Gone' was always earmarked as our production piece," DeLorenzo says. "We were always gonna fill that one out and build it piece by piece rather than try to go for a basic take with the three of us playing our instruments. It was built from the bottom up."

The drum track started with brushes on the snare drum, then DeLorenzo added overdubs of cymbal, tambourine, and bass drum. Unusually, though, the bass drum—the only bass drum that appears on the whole album—is played on the downbeat, as opposed to the one and three of the measures, which would be the traditional placement for the instrument in most popular music.

"It's just the way that the song was presenting itself to me," DeLorenzo says. "And it's just part of our quirkiness. It's just the way that we heard things."

Also unusual is the fact that the bass drum was a Scotch marching drum, the type carried by parading drummers who play with mallets. The drum is much larger in diameter than the standard bass drum you might see as part of a set. And once again, Ritchie was the source of this unusual instrument, after finding it in the same place as his xylophone.

"The bass drum?" he says. "I found it on the street."

The guitar, bass, and vocal tracks on "Gone Daddy Gone" remained in keeping with the rest of the album's recording approach. For the overdubs, though, Van Hecke thought Ritchie could firm up the xylophone part.

"I was improvising that solo every time," Ritchie says, "and Mark said, 'You can't just improvise all the time, sometimes you have to compose something.' So he asked me to actually write a solo, and so if you listen to it, you can hear it's composed. Even now I play it the same."

It's a solo that's so catchy and bold that, outside of the jazz greats, it might be the best-known xylophone solo in the history of popular music. Not that I can think of many other examples of xylophone solos in pop music, but Ritchie isn't here to disagree.

"I think it might be the most prominent mallet part on a popular recording," he says.

The band briefly trades twos after the solo—a jazz practice in which each instrument improvises individually for two measures at a time—and then the xylophone drops out completely for the third verse, in which Gano sings a four-line phrase quoted directly from the Muddy Waters song "I Just Want to Make Love to You"—which, unbeknownst to Gano at the time, was actually a song written by Willie Dixon.

"I know I had heard the Muddy Waters version of it," he says. "But I'm not sure if I'd heard Willie Dixon's yet or not at that point."

It wasn't something he gave much thought to. "Gone Daddy Gone" had already been written without the Dixon verse; it was just something Gano had started dropping in live.

"It seemed to work in an unexpected kind of crazy way," he says, "and I thought, you know, this is a nice addition to the song and kind of a tribute."

By the time it came time to record, the verse had become such a standard part of the song's live performance that Gano asked Van Hecke if it would be a problem to record it.

"He said, there's no problem with that because it's not long enough," Gano says. "Just you can do it and don't worry about it. And he was completely wrong. It was terrible advice." Eventually realizing the song needed proper attribution, the band added Willie Dixon as a co-writer.

"When it came to me years later, I felt terrible about it," Gano says, "and so we worked out something, and that's fine." His inadvertent sample from so many years ago brought with it an unexpected benefit, though. "It's an honor to have co-written a song with Willie Dixon," he says, chuckling. "But it's not the way it should have happened."

Before the track was even recorded, DeLorenzo says that there was an understanding it would probably be the album's single. "It was always designed as a production piece and was going to be the stand-out on the record," he says, "so we were always thinking that it might be the single from the record, because it sounds the most normal in a way."

"Slash said they wanted it to be the single because it had bass drum on it," Ritchie says, adding, "We thought it should have been 'Blister in the Sun.'"

I mention to Ritchie that the bass drum isn't even played in the "normal" bass drum spots, and so it seems funny to me that the instrument would have played into Slash's marketing plan at all.

"It's impossible to know why Slash made the decisions that they made," he says, but then adds that he's sure *why* so many of their decisions were perplexing. "Because they were on drugs," he says. "At least the owner was."

TRACK TEN: GOOD FEELING

"With some of the songs on this record," Victor DeLorenzo says, "you're not exactly sure if the person singing it is going to get out alive."

A guy is going to hack it apart. A guy is ready to take a bow and say goodnight. A guy knows what it's like to hate way down deep inside. The city's restless, it's ready to pounce. The love is gone. A blister is blistering. The whole album is a catalogue of tensions like this—existential and romantic and dramatic—with each song's narrator seeming like at any moment he might crack.

"But this particular song," DeLorenzo says, "it's an optimistic song, and it leaves you, not to be coy, but it leaves you with a good feeling."

He is, of course, talking about "Good Feeling," the tenth and final track on *Violent Femmes*, a tender and poignant three-minute-and-fifty-three-second meditation on ephemerality and the passage of time that, incredibly, was written by Gordon Gano in 1978 when he was only fifteen years old.

"It was always probably obvious to all of us," Gano says. "Close the album with that."

"It resolves so many emotions," Brian Ritchie says. "It makes you feel like, ahhhhh."

"And also, it just throws another curve at the listener thinking, well, how can they do something like 'To the Kill' and then play this?" DeLorenzo says. "But that's one of the wonderful things about the Femmes is that we were prepared to go any direction at any time."

The album's second big production number after "Gone Daddy Gone," "Good Feeling" sees the band expanding to twenty-four-track recording again (as on "Gone Daddy Gone"), with DeLorenzo playing brushes on a full drum set, and piano and violin appearing for the first and only times on the album. Van Hecke played the piano, and Gano the violin. It was an arrangement the band worked out in preproduction at Van Hecke's house.

"Mark had a piano in his front room," DeLorenzo says. "So we just gathered around the piano there and just played through the song a few times." It didn't take long for the parts to come together. And while Van Hecke has an advanced degree in orchestral conducting and extensive training on the piano, Gano's skills on the violin—which he played in high school—were more rudimentary.

"That was just me doing it the best I could," Gano says of his performance, which matches the tenderness of his vocal delivery with a pared down melody stretching out languidly over eight bars. It was a solo Van Hecke pushed Gano to write.

"Gordon had an initial idea, which wasn't a good idea," Van Hecke says, explaining that Gano had planned to simply play the same melody as his vocal line. "I thought, that's not going to work. That's your solo?" Together, with Van Hecke on a xylophone and Gano on the violin, they worked up the new part.

"It's so simple, but it's just so poignant," DeLorenzo says, "and Mark plays some beautiful piano on there. Brian's bass, the beautiful little solo section … And then I love the end with the voices."

The very simple la-la vocal hook in the end "is actually very complex" Ritchie says, and then he sings it for a second, locating the exact complication in question: one measure in the middle of the phrase that departs from the song's 4/4 time signature.

"It was actually years later that it came to my awareness that there was something unusual about the time signature there," Gano says. "To me, it was just utter simplicity. And I remember the first time somebody was joining in and not following and messing it up. And it was like, wow, isn't this the simplest thing? And it's like, well, actually, it's not."

"Gordon didn't know the rules," Ritchie says.

Once again, Gano chalks up his lack of experience as an asset in having written the part, but there's another portion of the song that was written around the same time that he's grateful now to have cut. The instrumental section of the song, he explains, uses a few different chords that don't appear elsewhere, and the reason for that, he says, "is because I had originally written that section as a kind of a bridge and there were words through that whole part, or through the section where it changes the chord, and I am so glad and so grateful that I edited it out. I don't think anybody's heard it, because it would have destroyed the song. Just ruined it."

Gano starts thinking about the old part, and then, as if under great duress, says, "Oh my gosh. It's in my head … it's so wrong, so wrong for the song."

The section apparently involved a series of words that held hidden meaning—the "real" meaning of what the song was about, Gano says—which could only be revealed to you if you solved a type of word puzzle.

"It involved something very cryptic," Gano says, "which was like changing letters around, so that this is like a mystery word, but only I know the secret of what it really means."

He groans in pain.

"I guess you're not going to tell me any of the lyrics, are you?" I say.

"You are correct," Gano says. "I've said too much already."

The song ends with one final chord on the piano, which Van Hecke lets ring out while holding the sustain pedal down with his foot, and for a second or two it seems like the note might just linger forever, until with one tiny little click, you hear Van Hecke's foot relax and the pedal clacks back into place. With that, *Violent Femmes* is complete.

The area of a vinyl LP closest to the center has the lowest sonic fidelity because the grooves there have less room to accommodate audio information, so simply because of real estate, it is the region best suited for quieter songs. This logic alone meant that "Good Feeling" would work best as the album's final track, something the band understood, but much more importantly, they felt the song was the perfect moment on which to end.

When CDs came out, though, and the idea of sequencing an album became less rigidly defined by physical confines, *Violent Femmes* was released with two bonus tracks—"Ugly" and "Give Me the Car," both of which were recorded for a UK single in 1983. These songs follow immediately after "Good Feeling" on the CD, but because they employ more electrified instrumentation and aggressive production than the rest of the album, the perfection of the original sequencing takes a sharp turn.

"It was great to get those songs out and have people be able to hear them along with the CD," Gano says. "But it totally destroyed the idea of the album being a whole piece that ends with 'Good Feeling.' With the CD, 'Good Feeling' ends, and then it's like, bang! Here's a punk rock thing." To Gano, *Violent Femmes* ends with "Good Feeling," and there's nothing that can change that. "It has to be the original album order, beginning to end," he says. "That's the way we intended it."

5

Release and Success

"I just found a letter that I'd saved," Gordon Gano says. "It was written some years ago. I still have it, because it was so heartfelt. The person who wrote it said that they had a younger brother who had been diagnosed with a condition and given certain medications, which now are not given, and that he died of those medications when he was a teenager. And they said that they buried him with a *Violent Femmes* cassette tape." He pauses for a second. "I'm getting choked up, just saying that. It was because he listened to the tape so much that they buried it with him, because it brought him so much joy."

Those *Violent Femmes* cassettes, they were important in this way, like little talismans passed around for years in some type of initiation rite, magic magnetic containers for all that we were feeling and thinking and thinking we might one day feel. So it doesn't seem unusual at all to me that one family might imagine the band's debut album could bring joy to their loved one in another dimension. God knows it did in this one. Circulating with the kind of provenance you never forget—with sources like "my babysitter with blue nail polish," "Steve Brackbill's older sister," "my cousin Andy," "my older brother Rush, who played it in his orange TR-7 convertible," and "Little Mike who put it on a mixtape for me when I was fifteen"—*Violent Femmes* established itself as a viral musical sensation over the span of a decade, a swell of influence that started in 1983, when the album came out, and peaked around 1991, when it hit the Billboard 200 for the first time and was certified platinum. Before it could do any of those things, though, the record had to be released. And for that to happen, the band still needed a record deal.

"The finished album, the one that you hear now, it was already mixed and everything," says Brian Ritchie. "And we sent it around to many many labels again."

Things did not go well.

"I recall nothing other than just total rejections and being ignored," says Gano.

Some rejections came from major labels, but the band targeted smaller ones too, like the tiny Los Angeles punk outfit Slash Records, an offshoot of *Slash* magazine, which Van Hecke first learned about in the pages of *The Isthmus*, an independent newspaper out of Madison, Wisconsin, which ran an interview with Bob Biggs, Slash's president. Van Hecke, who by this point had become the Violent Femmes' manager as well as producer, read the interview and liked what Biggs had to say. He suggested DeLorenzo send him an album.

"Why did I have Victor do it?" he says. "Just to have it come from a band member. I thought that might get a better reaction."

Anna Statman, an A&R rep at Slash, wrote back to say that she was interested, but ultimately Biggs rejected the signing.

"And then, sometime later," Gano says, "I don't know how long it was, their answer changed to yes. We asked Bob Biggs, the president, we said, what changed? And he said he got tired of coming to work every day and hearing the people who worked there playing the music of the band that he had rejected."

It turns out that two employees at Slash—including Statman, the A&R rep who'd initially expressed interest— simply loved *Violent Femmes* so much that they kept playing the album at work, even though the label had rejected it.

"So basically," Gano says, "in a way, Bob Biggs was saying, I don't think you guys are good. I don't think you guys have a future or a chance. But just because I'm sick of it, I'm going to sign you."

At long last, the Violent Femmes had what they had been striving for: a record label willing to sign them. The terms of the offer that Slash eventually made, though, were not what the band had been dreaming of.

"It was like, no advance," Ritchie says. "Tiny royalty in perpetuity."

"One attorney said they had never seen a worse contract for an artist in their whole career," Gano says. "And we knew it was bad, but nobody else was saying they would put this thing out. It was just, if we wanted to get things going, the answer was going to be yes. So we said yes, and I think that it was the right business decision. I mean, it's easier to say that now, but I felt like that at the time. So it was, I think, essential for us to say yes to Slash, even though it was a terrible deal."

The contract was signed. A release date was put on the calendar: April 13, 1983. The album still needed a cover, though. The band wanted to use a collage that their friend Geoff "Stinky" Worman had put together, featuring children on the street playing different instruments, but Statman, now the band's official A&R rep at Slash, wouldn't accept it. Van Hecke, who loved the collage, was frustrated. "So I said, what the fuck do you want?" he says, and then went to the Slash offices in Los Angeles to work it all out. He sat down with Statman, and together they just started flipping through magazines, searching for inspiration.

"The style of the time was new wave," Van Hecke says, "and Violent Femmes flew in the face of that," so they looked for something that played against type. The idea of having a child on the cover, he says, represented the idea of an introduction, of first sight, and naivete. Clearly, this visual metaphor also involved loss of innocence, something percolating in so many of Gano's songs, and when Statman found an image of a young girl that she liked, they agreed to hire a photographer to create something similar.

"We wanted a little girl peeking in the window of a garage," Van Hecke says. "The photographer got hold of a space in Hollywood. It was just a falling-apart garage. And he found this little girl, Billie Jo Campbell." Billie Jo had been walking down the street with her mother one day when the photographer, Ron Hugo, approached and asked Campbell's mother if she might be willing to let her daughter appear in the photoshoot. Campbell's mother, a "free spirit," as Billie Jo has described her, agreed.

"I was there at the shoot," Van Hecke says, "and I remember the little girl, Billie Jo, was barefoot. She was always getting cold. So in between shots I'd hold her feet."

Hugo kept telling Billie Jo that there were animals inside the garage, so that she'd look in the windows.

"I didn't know why they were making me look in this building," Billie Jo said years later, in the British publication *Stool Pigeon*. "I had no idea there were photographers there. I was … pissed off that I couldn't see the animals and I was all cranky by the end of it."

The cajoling worked, though, and eventually Hugo captured the photo he'd been aiming for: Billie Jo looking into the window of the dilapidated building, vines hanging around her, the paint peeling off the walls.

"When we first saw it, we weren't too sure," DeLorenzo says. "But then it started to grow on me. The delicate quality, the youthfulness …."

Van Hecke came around to the cover too, but at the time, he had more urgent concerns than whether or not the image was to his liking. "I thought, I just have to accept it to get things done," he says.

DeLorenzo remembers the first time he saw the final product. "I was holding the vinyl copy of the first Violent Femmes album in my left hand, and in my right hand, I was holding my newborn baby son, Malachi," he says. "So I was thinking, ok, here's my future right in front of me. Here's my son and here's my band. I hope we can make this work."

Gano too recalls how he felt when he first saw the record, saying that the moment filled him with "an incredible sense of creation, of something that's coming out of the void. The feeling of, this is like a dream. It's like, it's actually happening right now when you put that needle down and you hear it start to happen."

After all of the buildup, though, *Violent Femmes'* release date was a muted affair.

"There wasn't an official album release show," DeLorenzo says. "In Milwaukee, we were the weird people that played on the street. So, the idea of having a record release party, that idea just did not exist. Eventually, we came to represent Milwaukee all over the world, but at that particular time, we were just known to ourselves and to a few of our friends."

Early reviews began to roll in. They were good. In *Rolling Stone*, J. D. Considine gave the album four stars, saying it was an "unnervingly precocious debut of a Milwaukee trio that not only acts like it just reinvented rock & roll but somehow manages to sound like it as well." In the *Village Voice*, Robert Christgau compared Gano positively to Jonathan Richman, a similarity that *Creem* noted too. Mention of Lou Reed as an influence was also common, and by the time the album had only been out for a month, the band did an interview with the *LA Weekly* in which Gano said, "Someone was talking to me earlier and asked, 'Are you getting sick of people always comparing you to … ' And there was this pause, and I just knew, 'Lou Reed, Jonathan Richman'—and I realized that, yes, I am sick of it. And I haven't been before. But today I am sick of it. Which is a breakthrough of sorts. So I guess now I'll start getting hostile." Clearly Gano wasn't too serious, though, because he then added, "I always take it as a compliment."

Van Hecke arranged for a cross-country tour. "We weren't making much money," he says, "but the point was you play this little club and the owner will want to publicize it, and he'll get a write-up in the local paper … " It was the classic formula for building grassroots support. "The main point of the business at that point was just to get more notoriety," DeLorenzo says. "So we were just trying to play anywhere and everywhere in the USA."

The band toured Europe for two months after their US dates, and when they returned, the fruits of their labor had begun to appear. Slash had released "Gone Daddy Gone" as a single, and though it hadn't done much at first, by the time the band was back in the States, a few tiny stations—like WMSE at the Milwaukee School of Engineering and WZMD at Illinois State University in Normal, Illinois—had started "playing the hell out of it," DeLorenzo says. "And once we started breaking through on college radio and the record was getting a good response from people there, then it started to take off and people wanted to hear about us and have us come play in clubs, and then we started getting into smaller theaters, and then we played on college campuses … For the longest time, though, we were just prepared to play anywhere, anytime, anyplace."

Violent Femmes continued to gain traction nationally, even while the band forged ahead with new work. *Hallowed Ground*, their second album, was released only one year later, in 1984, and the Jerry Harrison-produced *The Blind Leading the Naked* followed suit in 1986. Both albums made an impact, but it was nothing compared to the first album, which just continued to build momentum as it spread via word-of-mouth among listeners. In 1987, *Violent Femmes* finally went gold, after which another new album, *3*, was released, yet still the debut continued to outsell the rest of the catalog. By 1991, when the album was certified platinum— the same year that the Violent Femmes' fifth album *Why Do Birds Sing?* was released—*Violent Femmes'* unusually drawn-out success had created an odd confusion among listeners about just when the album had actually been made.

"I remember meeting somebody who said you're the ultimate, great, perfect nineties band," Gano says. "And I'm thinking, you know, we started at the beginning of the eighties, and the album everybody loves came out in the early eighties, and yet it's like, you're the ultimate best nineties band? I realized that it was because that's when they got into the band. That's when the band existed for them."

Another reason listeners were confused about the album's origin was because of the overwhelming prevalence of cassette copies dubbed onto blanks. These things were everywhere. Maxwell, TDK, Sony, Bosch, all with handwritten labels—

if any at all—that often made it impossible not only to tell when the album had been released, but even what its title was. My friend Shannon, the one who bought that acoustic bass guitar with the credit card he found on the sidewalk, had a dubbed copy that he says he listened to every day for weeks, only to then discover the second side. It was like finding a whole new album. Gordan Gano remembers a conversation he had once with a fan that sums up well this state of affairs.

"This was in the late eighties or early nineties," Gano says. "The fan was all excited about meeting me, and then he said, Can I ask you one question? I said, Sure. And he said, I love your first album. What does the cover look like? I've never seen it. I've only seen it on cassette tapes that people had at parties that they had made."

Add to all this the band's acoustic instrumentation and a recording approach that aimed to recreate Elvis's Sun Studio sessions, and *Violent Femmes* presented a lasting audio mystery.

"There's nothing that identifies it with a particular time period with how it was recorded," Gano says. "It could have been done in any of these other decades and eras, or it could be done just like that now, if somebody wanted to."

"We intentionally avoided every trapping of the time," says Ritchie, "and we even avoided a lot of rock conventions in general. So that meant that the music was outside of time. It's ahead of the time, but it's also outside of time. It could have even been behind the time—the album could have probably come out in the fifties. I mean, we didn't do anything on that album that you couldn't have done in the fifties. To me the album is timeless as a recording, simply because it didn't use any cliches of the time that it was in."

Though technical aspects are surely a part of the reason listeners have connected to *Violent Femmes* for so long, they aren't the only ones. Stylistic and performance choices can only play so big of a role in how a song is received. At the root is always the song itself, and the songwriter.

"I think the main factor is Gordon's vulnerability in the lyrics," Ritchie says. "He had a persona which a lot of people were just thinking, holy shit, he's saying everything that I'm thinking, but I would never have the guts to say. And he's doing it really well."

We take for granted today that someone like Rivers Cuomo or Ezra Koenig might become a rock icon, but this was not always the case. Gano was a progenitor of the ironic outsider rock antihero, a persona that stood out in the landscape of the early eighties.

"Look back forty-plus years," Ritchie says. "There were no rock stars who were not trying to be cool, you know. Even the dorkiest rock star was still trying to be cool. So Gordon's vulnerability and his lack of trying to be macho and trying to impress women in the usual kind of groin ways was a big part of it."

Gano, for his part, defers any focus on himself and says that the album's staying power is rooted in the joy that it gives people. "Before we recorded," he says, "we were playing songs on the street. The people that responded the most were little kids and much older people. There's something in the bounce, the energy of the music that connects, I think, with kids. There's certainly a timeless aspect to it."

In the end, though, Ritchie says the album's popularity isn't that complicated.

"The music is good," he says, "it kicks ass, and it's catchy."

As of this writing, *Violent Femmes* has sold more than 7 million copies. Its songs have become classics of contemporary American music. You can hear them across the globe, in sports stadiums, in television and film, on headphones and radios and in the hands of other bands performing their own interpretations. "And the thing about this record is that it has never stopped," says Jeff Castelaz, former president of Elektra Records and now Violent Femmes' manager. "It just keeps going and going. The licensing … Streaming is huge … " And while not a single track off the album has ever reached the *Billboard* charts, Castelaz says that songs like those on *Violent Femmes* end up having a bigger and more lasting impact than any flash in the pan. "I call these kinds of songs *cultural* hits," he says. "And the cool thing about the kinds of artists who have cultural hits is that, generally speaking, they work harder, and they're grateful for the audience-artist connection those songs have created over the years and decades. Smash hits are disposable. An album like *Violent Femmes* becomes a friend who stays with you for your life."

One possible drawback of having written an album full of cultural hits, though, is the strange professional burden of having to play those songs for the rest of your life. It's a problem the members of Violent Femmes unilaterally dismiss. Not only do they say that they still connect to the material because of the quality of the songs themselves, but they also appreciate the connections listeners have made to them over the decades, connections that Ritchie compares to his own life.

"When I go to a Rolling Stones concert, and they play 'Satisfaction,'" he says, and then leans forward, as if to emphasize what he's getting ready to say next, "I like it."

I ask Gano what type of success the band expected for themselves in 1983, before the album was released, back when they were still just a trio of young men playing street corners and dreaming of all that might come to pass.

"I think we would have thought we would have been either a lot bigger or a whole lot smaller," Gano says. He describes the type of success punk bands enjoy as one model Violent Femmes saw for themselves, along the lines of what Johnny Thunders, Richard Hell and the Voidoids, and Television were doing. "Playing to a couple of hundred people in New York and LA and London," Gano says. "Putting records out on a little indie punk label and maybe getting in a van and going across the country to play in any town that has a punk club. That's success." Another option, he says, lies on the opposite end of the spectrum. "It's either that, or you're playing a stadium. That's all that we would have known or thought. So, in a sense, what we've done for so long now is between those two. It's not even close to either of them. It's like rock middle class." He considers it all for a second, then adds, "Sometimes I've thought, we're the most popular unknown band."

There have been times when, just for a moment, Gano says that even he didn't know his own band.

"Once, maybe twice, I felt like in the distance I heard something, and I knew that I liked it," he says. "And then, when I zeroed in on it, I realized that it was our first album. And how cool is it that my first thought was: this sounds great."

Epilogue: In Dreams Begin Responsibilities

I did the math while filling up at a gas station. Twenty-six. That's how many years it had been since I'd last seen the Violent Femmes play. In those years, I'd gone bald, gotten married, had a child, and published four books. But back then—in 1998, when I last saw the band—I was a 21-year-old drummer with a full head of hair and a band with a minor hit song who had just shared the stage with the Violent Femmes at a music festival in Atlanta. My band went on well before them that day, a totally unplanned alignment, but today I was on my way back to Atlanta, this time to see them on purpose.

I holstered the gas nozzle and merged onto I-85.

"It's not a regular show," Chris Phillips had said when I asked him for tickets. Phillips is part of the Violent Femmes' management team and a close old friend of mine. He was worried that I wouldn't get a chance to see the band in the "right" way, since this was going to be one of their symphony shows—something they've done in several major markets in recent years, including Milwaukee, where in 2023 they recorded a special for PBS. I didn't tell Chris that that's exactly why I'd picked this show, as a direct response to Gordon Gano's warning that I shouldn't come see the band at all because he was worried that I'd be disappointed in all the ways in which their live shows are unlike the debut album. With the addition of the symphony, I thought, this show *couldn't* be like the album. It would allow me to lower my expectations completely. If I was being honest, though, that wasn't the only reason I'd picked the show. I think I was also hoping that the symphony part meant I'd have better odds of getting to bed early.

I play this game sometimes: I try to imagine a concert I'd like to go to. Any concert. Any musician. Anywhere. Somehow, I still hope I might find an answer, but the truth is usually I can't. As a musician who toured for so many years, I think I've just clocked too many hours inside of clubs and theaters for much easy magic to still be found there. Not that I don't appreciate the Violent Femmes' ability to perform on a stage. In a way, I think they are probably best live. Listen to some of the bonus tracks on the fortieth anniversary edition of *Violent Femmes*, like the live version of "Special" from the Beaneth-It-All Café in 1981, and you can hear the heady energy in the room, like a whole new world is being created and they're all discovering it in there together. I think there's even an argument that the Violent Femmes' debut album holds up so well because it is, in many ways, a live recording.

But part of what I'm getting at is that I didn't much care one way or another if I saw the band live. I'd done all the interviews I needed for this book. I knew the album inside out. A live show wasn't required. I've written for long enough, though, to know that it's smart to see your subjects in person. To report live from the scene. To find the right details and, if not make yourself part of the story, at least give yourself a chance to talk to it.

I rolled down the interstate, thinking about all the things I'd discuss with the band. I'd give them an update on the book's schedule. Fix the spelling of some names. Fact-check a few things about Milwaukee clubs. And then in a flash, I remembered a conversation I'd had with Gano a few months before, about Lou Reed. Reed—who Gano has always cited as a major influence and with whom he collaborated on a 2002 solo album—once told Gano that, for a while at least, he was requesting that any journalist wanting to speak with him first read a short story written by Delmore Schwartz called "In Dreams Begin Responsibilities." Schwartz, a titan of twentieth-century American poetry, had been Reed's professor at Syracuse, and Reed had idolized Schwartz, probably in the same manner Gano felt about Reed. Reed's point in asking writers to read the Schwartz story, Gano had said, was that "if you're not going to take just a few minutes to read this short story, which was very meaningful to him, it's like, why are we even talking?" Gano thought Reed might have even quizzed writers about it. I made a joke about being an English professor and yet never having read the story myself, after which Gano said, "You should maybe read it."

This part of our conversation lasted maybe one minute, and we'd spoken for hours that day. But what if Gano remembered that one minute, I thought. What if he asked me about the story?

I downloaded a copy at the hotel. I didn't have much time before I needed to leave for Symphony Hall. Maybe twenty minutes. I called an Uber and started to read.

Shwartz's story (I kept thinking, *this was written in 1937?* Incredibly modern, oh my god) is about a man in a theater watching a film about how his parents met. Everyone else is watching like it's a regular movie, but somehow the narrator understands that what he's seeing is essentially a magical live feed of the past. The story is a technical tour de force. The mood is bleak. The prose is spare. Eventually, just after the narrator's father proposes to his mother onscreen, the narrator screams out, "Don't do it. It's not too late to change your minds."

I couldn't tell if this was a story about the dangers of looking back or if it was a story about the inability to change the past. Either way, it brought to mind Gano's warning about not coming to see them perform. Maybe Gano was right, I thought. Maybe I had only come to Atlanta as part of a doomed quest to revisit my youth.

Uber notified me that Miloslav had arrived in a blue Tesla 3.

"Is music bother you, you don't mind?" he said as I got in. He was playing Slavic yacht rock.

"No, it's fine," I said.

I kept thinking about Schwartz's story as we drove away, wondering if it was an omen, warning me to turn back.

There are certain places where people don't look their best. The airport. The DMV. Walmart. A dressing room at Marshalls. Add to that list, perhaps, the well-lit lobby of Symphony Hall in Atlanta before a Violent Femmes concert. I entered with a couple of old-timers in tight black jeans and big guts. Inside were more men in the same jeans with the same guts, all milling around. There was a white guy with dreadlocks in his early fifties wearing cargo shorts. I started wondering, am I one of these people? In the bathroom, I looked in the mirror. I was a bald 47-year-old white guy in a dark blue shirt and black jeans. I didn't have a gut, at least. Then behind me, another bald middle-aged guy walked by. He too was wearing a dark blue shirt and black jeans and didn't have a gut. He didn't look so good. He looked like me.

Back in the lobby, an older man yelled, "Hey, nice Cramps shirt!" as he tottered past, and then the guy with the Cramps shirt cracked a huge smile and waved. Maybe we all *were* looking our best, I thought. Maybe this was as good as it got. Not every band gets to last long enough to see their fan base reach and even pass middle age. I guess this is what it looks like when you put out a record in 1983 and it remains a cultural touchstone.

Inside the theater, three tiers of red velvet seats rose to a chandeliered ceiling. *Disney's Frozen in Concert* was advertised on a large projection above the stage. Everyone around me seemed exceedingly kind. There was great excitement. Much merchandise had been purchased. But I don't know. Maybe I'd sabotaged the whole thing. Gano's warning, which had only been a joke, I'd let grow into stupid importance. And now that Schwartz story had me spooked. Once the band started playing, I wondered, was I too going to start screaming, like Schwartz's protagonist, telling the Violent Femmes that it wasn't too late to stop?

I'm happy to report that no, I didn't scream any insane commands at the band. In fact, I just sat there calmly as they put on their show. But maybe my whole scheme to avoid expectation had worked too well, because even though the Violent Femmes' performance was excellent, all I did was compute and analyze. I remained in my seat like a Violent Femmes scientist, detached and emotionless.

Afterward, I found myself standing backstage in a brightly lit room near the man who now plays drums for the Violent Femmes. DeLorenzo left the band years ago. I felt pretty confident that I knew this new drummer's name—I follow him on Instagram—and I didn't want to be rude, so I turned and said, "Hi, are you Jason?"

"No," he said, and then he just looked at me. He didn't say another word.

"Oh," I said, "Sorry."

I guess I'd been wrong about knowing his name.

The rest of the band and crew rolled in. Other people too. Someone brought a hideous cake. There was one guy who was super fit and cool looking and wearing leather pants and somehow pulling them off with ease. He looked like more of a rock star than anyone in the building. Turns out he was one of the bass players from the symphony. It was a weird scene. These things always are. I spoke to Brian Ritchie briefly, thanking him for his help with this project, and then basically just hung out with the tour bus driver until the road manager told me I could stick my head into the small room where Gano was holed up.

"Hey," I said, stepping into the door frame. "I'm Nic Brown, the guy writing the 33 1/3 book. ... "

"Nic!" Gano said. He seemed honestly pleased to see me. We'd only ever spoken on the phone. Two of his friends were in there with him, and Gano introduced me as if I was already one of them. We spoke amongst ourselves for maybe twenty seconds before Gano said, "So hey, did you ever read that Delmore Schwartz story?"

A rush of satisfaction shot through me, like I'd studied just the right equation for a pop quiz.

"Yes," I said.

Gano's friends raised their eyebrows, curious, and so I explained the whole thing about Lou Reed's homework for writers, but then they looked even more curious, so I told them what the story was about. I didn't go into detail, or mention that I'd only read the thing a couple of hours earlier, I just gave the type of perfect recap that could only have happened with the story still fresh in my mind. I described it with feeling. It might have been the best retelling of a story I've ever given. My whole performance lasted only a few sentences, but they were the perfect few sentences, and when

I got to the scene where the narrator yells at his parents, the power of the story left my body and entered everyone else in the room. It was as if a thread had been drawn straight from Schwartz to Reed to Gano to me and now back to him and his friends. Or maybe I was the only one feeling this way.

But then Gano said, "I just got goosebumps!"

And that's when I knew what I had come to Atlanta for.

I've tried to push away bias while writing this book. To act like I'm not just a fan. But it's hard to smother love, and backstage with Gano and his pals, I think I was reminded of why I started this whole project to begin with: because *Violent Femmes* is an album I love, and writing is an exercise in connection. It was probably the same reason Lou Reed wanted people to read that Delmore Schwartz story in the first place: to share a connection through art. And in much the same way a formative teacher might continue to influence a student over the years—as Schwartz did for Reed—*Violent Femmes* has set a compass point in my life, directing my aesthetic sensibilities ever since I first heard it on that fateful afternoon in Doug Starr's house at age eleven. So even though I had already connected to Gano via his music, when I retold Shwartz's story to him and his friends backstage in Atlanta's Symphony Hall that night, I felt like I'd made a new and unexpected link, a brief little personal one, and the Violent Femmes fan in me loved it. Sharing a goosebump-inducing moment with Gordon Gano via a short story recommended by Lou Reed is about as good as it gets.

We didn't talk for much longer. I sort of felt like, probably best to just leave it at that. I thanked Gano for his time and left.

Back at the hotel, I got a whiskey from the bar, went up to my room, and put on the Dodgers game. It was the eighth inning. The Dodgers were down by six. The crowd was losing interest. But then the organist played "Blister in the Sun" and for a second, everyone seemed to perk up. Together they all clapped their hands, and then they did it again and again and again. It was the sound of something they couldn't resist.

Acknowledgments

The author would like to thank Gordon Gano, Victor DeLorenzo, Brian Ritchie, Mark Van Hecke, Chris Phillips, Jeff Castelaz, Shannon Ferguson, Kacey Nicosia, Nat Jacks, boice-Terrel Allen, Michael Azerrad, Logan and Maria Brown, Rosecrans Baldwin, and Frances and Abby Brown.

Sources

Unless otherwise indicated, all quotes are from interviews conducted by the author between August 2024 and May 2025.